AMBER

A WINTER GATHERING

TWENTY-ONE PIECES
+ ONE

by Kim Hargreaves

DESIGNS
Kim Hargreaves

PHOTOGRAPHY
Graham Watts

STYLING
Kim Hargreaves

HAIR & MAKE-UP
Diana Fisher

MODELS
Amanda Hinchcliffe, Sally Mitchell,
Louise Güntert, Nichola Radcliffe & Hannah Wright

EDITOR
Kathleen Hargreaves

EDITORIAL DESIGN
Graham Watts

LAYOUTS
Angela Lin

PATTERNS
Sue Whiting & Stella Smith

LOCATION
Cliffe House
Tel: 01484 222720
E-mail: office.cliffhouse@kirklees-schools.org.uk

BRITISH LIBRARY CATALOGUING IN PUBLICATION DATA
A catalogue record for this book is available from the British Library.

ISBN-10: 1-906487-03-4
ISBN-13: 978-1-906487-03-4

CONTENTS

5

THE
DESIGNS

Good friends gather for a fun country house weekend. As winter envelops they are found wearing the season's rich shades to dramatic effect, the inspiration for these magical colours is taken from mythical potions of luscious berries, herbs and spices. The garments have an air of self assured style —from cosy and snug to sleek and elegant— carrying with them a wealth of texture, from delicate lace to glorious cables. The grand hall and secret gardens provide the perfect setting for such an enchanting collection...

THE GLORIOUS COUNTRY
HOUSE PROVIDES THE
PERFECT BACKDROP
Hannah is wearing CLARA,
a long-line waistcoat with
pocket detail.

9

BOHO STYLE, COMBINE
FLIRTY CHIFFON WITH A
CHUNKY WRAP JACKET
Amanda is wearing OCTAVIA,
a belted jacket with
lush collar.

THIS PAGE
A FEATHERED HEADDRESS
TOPS A SNUG CAPE
Hannah wears CHARITY
which fastens with a single button.
OPPOSITE
TEAL BLUE HIGHLIGHTS
WINTER'S RUSSET TONES
Louise wears SOUL,
a hat with beaded trim.

OPPOSITE
*VIBRANT COLOUR
COMPLIMENTS
EFFORTLESS GRACE*
Hannah is wearing PRUDENCE,
a sweater with an elegant drape.
THIS PAGE
*PRINTS CLASH IN
QUIRKY STYLE*
Louise wears SPLENDOUR,
a soft shrug with single button,
while Hannah is wearing CLARA.

17

OPPOSITE
A TRUE ENGLISH ROSE,
DEEP CABLES WORN
OVER RICH TAFFETA
Sally is wearing NELL
a belted jacket.
THIS PAGE
A SLOUCHY BEADED HAT
COMPLETES THE LOOK
Louise wears SOUL.

THIS PAGE
JOIN THE CLAN, TEAM
A PEPLUM JACKET WITH
THE SEASON'S TARTAN
Hannah wears PAISLEY, a
fitted jacket with cables.
OPPOSITE
KEEP IT SHORT
AND NEAT
Louise is wearing BELLA
shrug with a generous collar.

THIS PAGE
ANGEL WING SLEEVES
ADORN A CHIC STYLE
Amanda is wearing JEWEL,
a fitted cardigan.
OPPOSITE
ALL THE TRIMMINGS,
WITH BEADS AND BOWS
Hannah wears SOUL hat.

THIS PAGE
HUES OF BLUSH MINGLE
WITH WINTER BLOOMS
Nichola wears WHISPER,
an understated sweater
with flounce hemline.
OPPOSITE
PLAID AND PRINT
A STRIKING STATEMENT
Hannah is wearing JEWEL
cardigan with a classic
three quarter sleeve.

WRAP UP AGAINST
A WINTERY CHILL
Hannah wears BETH,
an A-line coat
complete with
oversized buttons.

OPPOSITE
A BEADED SCARF
ADDS THE IDEAL
FINISHING TOUCH
Sally is wearing TRINKET
worked in mohair and silk.
THIS PAGE
RICH AMBER TONES
BLAZE AGAINST
GLOSSY EVERGREEN
Nichola wears LIZZY, a
tunic with split neckline
and deep collar.

33

ALL THAT GLISTENS,
BEADS ACT LIKE WINTER'S
PRECIOUS JEWELS
Amanda wears BLOOM,
a pretty sweater with
buttoned trim.

43

OPPOSITE
MIX IT UP WITH SUMPTUOUS
STRIPES, SILK SCARF AND
TRADITIONAL TWEEDS
Amanda is wearing IVY,
a belted wrap waistcoat.
THIS PAGE
BEST OF FRIENDS
Nichola in LIZZY tunic, and
Hannah is wearing GINNY
fitted cardigan while
Amanda wears IVY waistcoat.

47

SULTRY SOPHISTICATION
SETS THE MOOD
Louise wears SPLENDOUR,
an elegant cardigan
worked cuff to cuff.

49

OPPOSITE
COBWEB FINE LACE WORKED
IN MOHAIR AND SILK
Nichola is wearing ALLURE,
a sweater with soft cowl neck.
THIS PAGE
SHELTERING FROM
THE SHOWERS
Hannah wears TRINKET,
a pretty beaded scarf.

51

THE
PATTERNS

ALLURE
LACY SWEATER WITH SOFT COWL NECK

Recommendation
Suitable for the more experienced knitter
Please see pages 1 & 50 for photographs.

	XS-S	S-M	M-L	XL-XXL	
To fit	**81-86**	**86-91**	**91-97**	**102-107**	cm
bust	32-34	34-36	36-38	40-42	in

Rowan Kidsilk Haze

	4	5	5	6	x 25gm

Photographed in Elegance

Needles
1 pair 2¾mm (no 12) (US 2) needles
1 pair 3¼ mm (no 10) (US 3) needles
1 pair 4 mm (no 8) (US 6) needles

Tension
19 sts and 31 rows to 10 cm measured over
lace pattern using 4 mm (US 6) needles.

Special abbreviations
ssk = Slip 1, K1, pass slip stitch over.
p2sso = Pass 2 slipped stitches over.
yo = yarn over (making 1 stitch)

BACK
Cast on 214 (234: 254: 278) sts using
2¾ mm (US 2) needles.
Row 1 (dec) (RS): K2tog, (K2tog, P2tog)
to last 4 sts, (K2tog) twice.
107 (117: 127: 139) sts.
Row 2: K1, (P1, K1) to end.
Row 3: K1, (K1, P1) to last 2 sts, K2.
Cont in rib as set until work measures 5 (5:
5.5: 5.5) cm, ending with a **RS** row.
Change to 4 mm (US 6) needles.
Next row (WS) (dec): P2 (3: 4: 2), (P2, P2tog)
26 (28: 30: 34) times, P1 (2: 3: 1).
81 (89: 97: 105) sts.
Rows 1 & 3 (RS): K1, * ssk, (K1, yo) twice,
K1, K2tog, K1, rep from * to end.
Row 2 & all WS rows: Purl.
Row 5: K1, * yo, ssk, K3, K2tog, yo, K1, rep
from * to end.
Row 7: K2, * yo, ssk, K1, K2tog, yo, K3, rep
from * ending last rep K2.
Row 9: K3, * yo, sl 2, K1, p2sso, yo, K5, rep
from *, ending last rep K3.
Row 10: Purl.
These 10 rows form the lace patt and are rep
throughout.
Keeping patt correct where possible and
taking rem sts into st st, shape sides as folls:
Dec 1 st at each end of next row 0 (1: 2: 3)
foll 6th rows, then on 7 (6: 5: 4) foll 4th rows.
65 (73: 81: 89) sts.
Work 13 rows.
Inc 1 st at each end of next row and foll 8th
row, then on every foll 6th row until there are
81 (89: 97: 105) sts.
Cont straight until back measures 40 (40:
41.5: 41.5), ending with a WS row.
Shape armholes
Cast off 4 sts at beg of next 2 rows.
73 (81: 89: 97) sts.
Dec 1 st at each end of next 3 (5: 5: 5)
rows, then on 2 (2: 3: 4) foll alt rows, then
on every foll 4th row until 61 (65: 71: 77)
sts rem.
Cont straight until armhole measures 18 (19:
20: 21) cm, ending with a WS row.

Shape shoulders and back neck
Cast off 5 (5: 6: 7) sts at beg of next 2 rows.
Cast off 5 (5: 5: 6) sts, patt until there are
8 (9: 10: 10) sts on right needle and turn,
leaving rem sts on a holder.
Cast off 4 sts, P to end.
Cast off rem 4 (5: 6: 6) sts.
With RS facing rejoin yarn to rem sts, cast off
centre 25 (27: 29: 31) sts, patt to end.
Complete to match first side, reversing
shaping.

FRONT
Work as given for back until front is 12 (14:
16: 18) rows shorter than back to start of
shoulder shaping, ending with a WS row.
Shape front neck
Patt 21 (23: 25: 27) sts and turn, leaving rem
sts on a holder.
Work each side of neck separately.
Dec 1 st at neck edge on next 4 (6: 4: 4) rows
and 3 (2: 4: 4) foll alt rows.
14 (15: 17: 19) sts.
Cont straight until front matches back to start
of shoulder shaping, ending with a WS row.
Shape shoulder
Cast off 5 (5: 6: 7) sts at beg of next row and
5 (5: 5: 6) sts at beg of foll alt row.
Work 1 row.
Cast off rem 4 (5: 6: 6) sts.
With RS facing rejoin yarn to rem sts, cast off
centre 19 (19: 21: 23) sts, patt to end.
Complete to match first side, reversing
shaping.

SLEEVES (both alike)
Cast on 151 (151: 169: 169) sts using
2¾ mm (US 2) needles.
Work lower edging as folls:
Row 1 (RS) (dec): K1, (yon, sl 2, K1, p2sso)
to end. 101 (101: 113: 113) sts.
Row 2: Purl.
Row 3: K1, (K2tog) to end.
51 (51: 57: 57) sts.
Row 4: Purl.
Cont in rib setting stitches as folls:

Next row (RS): K1, (K1, P1) to last 2 sts, K2.
Next row: K1, (P1, K1) to end.
Work 10 more rows in rib.
Keeping rib correct inc 1 st at each end of next row and foll 12th row.
55 (55: 61: 61) sts.
Cont in rib until work measures 8 (8: 8.5: 8.5) cm from start of rib, ending with a **RS** row.
Next row (WS): Work in rib, inc 10 (10: 12: 12) sts evenly across row.
65 (65: 73: 73) sts.
Change to 4 mm (US 6) and cont in lace patt as given for back and setting stitches as folls:
Rows 1 & 3 (RS): K1, * ssk, (K1, yo) twice, K1, K2tog, K1, rep from * to end.
Row 2 & all WS rows: Purl.
Row 5: K1, * yo, ssk, K3, K2tog, yo, K1, rep from * to end.
Row 6: Purl.
Keeping patt correct, shape sides as folls:
Dec 1 st at each end of next row and 6 (5: 6: 6) foll 4th rows, then on 0 (1: 1: 1) foll 6th row.
51 (51: 57: 57) sts.
Work 13 (15: 17: 17) rows, ending with a WS row.
Inc 1 st at each end of next row and 3 (3: 2: 4) foll 20th (20th: 28th: 14th) rows.
59 (59: 63: 67) sts.
Cont straight until sleeve measures 39 (40: 42: 44) cm from top of rib, ending with a WS row.

Shape sleeve top
Cast off 4 sts at beg of next 2 rows.
51 (51: 55: 59) sts.
Dec 1 st at each end of next 3 rows, then on 3 (2: 2: 1) foll alt rows.
39 (41: 45: 51) sts.
Work 3 rows.
Dec 1 st at each end of next row and 2 (3: 3: 4) foll 6th rows and then on 2 foll 4th rows, ending with a RS row.
29 (29: 33: 37) sts.
Work 1 row.

L & XL sizes only
Dec 1 st at each end of next row and 0 (1) foll alt row. 31 (33) sts.
Work 1 row.

All sizes
Dec 1 st at each end of next 4 rows.
21 (21: 23: 25) sts.
Cast off.

MAKING UP
Pin the pieces out, pulling gently to the correct size and shape. Using a steam iron, steam the pieces, but do not let the iron touch the knitting at all. Leave for a few seconds to cool, then complete as folls:
Use back stitch, or mattress stitch if preferred, join the shoulder seams.
Join sleeve and side seams.
Set sleeve top into armhole.

COLLAR
Cast on 292 (316: 337: 361) sts using 4 mm (US 6) needles.
Work edging as folls:
Row 1 (RS) (dec): K1 (yon, sl 2, K1, p2sso) to end.
195 (211: 225: 241) sts.
Row 2: Purl.
Row 3: K1, (K2tog) to end.
98 (106: 113: 121) sts.
Row 4: P to end, dec 1 st at end of row on **XS & S sizes only**.
97 (105: 113: 121) sts
Work in lace patt as given for back until collar measures 14 (15: 16: 17) cm from start of lace pattern.
Change to 3¼ mm (US 3) needles and cont for a further 7 (8: 9: 10) cm, ending with a WS row.
Cast off very loosely.
With RS facing, join the selvedges together.
With the **right side** of the sweater and **wrong side** of the collar facing, and matching the collar seam and the left shoulder seam, pin the collar evenly into place around the neck edging.
Sew the collar neatly into place around neck edge.

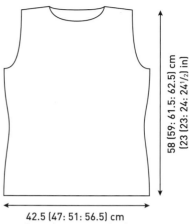

58 (59: 61.5: 62.5) cm
(23 (23: 24: 24½) in)

42.5 (47: 51: 56.5) cm
(16½ (18½: 20: 22) in)

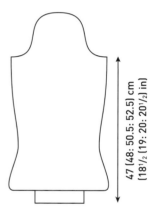

47 (48: 50.5: 52.5) cm
(18½ (19: 20: 20½) in)

LIZZY

UNSTRUCTURED TUNIC WITH SPLIT COLLAR

Recommendation

Suitable for the knitter with a little experience.
Please see pages 6, 33 & 42 for photographs.

	XS	S	M	L	XL	XXL	
To fit	**81**	**86**	**91**	**97**	**101**	**109**	cm
bust	32	34	36	38	40	43	in

Rowan Cocoon

| 6 | 7 | 8 | 9 | 10 | 11 x 100gm |

Photographed in Amber

Buttons – 3

Needles

1 pair 5 1/2mm (no 5) (US 9) needles
1 pair 6mm (no 4) (US 10) needles

Tension

14 sts and 22 rows to 10 cm measured over
pattern using 6mm (US 10) needles.

BACK

Cast on 62 (66: 72: 76: 80: 86) sts using
6mm (US 10) needles and work in patt as folls:
Foundation row (WS): P0 (0: 3: 0: 0: 3), K1
(3: 3: 1: 3: 3), *P4, K3; rep from * to last 5
(0: 3: 5: 0: 3) sts, P4 (0: 3: 4: 0: 3), K1 (0: 0:
1: 0: 0).
Cont in patt as folls:

XS, S, L and XL sizes
Row 1 (RS): P1 (3: ·: 1: 3: ·), *K2tog, (yfwd)
twice, sl 1, K1, psso, P3; rep from * to last 5
(7: ·: 5: 7: ·) sts, K2tog, (yfwd) twice, sl 1, K1,
psso, P1 (3: ·: 1: 3: 1).
Row 2: K1 (3: ·: 1: 3: ·), *P1, P into front
then back of double yfwd of previous row,
P1, K3; rep from * to last 5 (7: ·: 5: 7: ·) sts,
P1, P into front then back of double yfwd of
previous row, P1, K1 (3: ·: 1: 3: 1).
Row 3: P1 (3: ·: 1: 3: ·), *yon, sl 1, K1, psso,
K2tog, yfrn, P3; rep from * to last 5 (7: ·: 5:
7: ·) sts, yon, sl 1, K1, psso, K2tog, yfrn, P1
(3: ·: 1: 3: 1).
Row 4: K1 (3: ·: 1: 3: ·), *P4, K3; rep from * to
last 5 (7: ·: 5: 7: ·) sts, P4, K1 (3: ·: 1: 3: 1).
M and XXL sizes
Row 1 (RS): K1, yfwd, sl 1, K1, psso, P3,
*K2tog, (yfwd) twice, sl 1, K1, psso, P3; rep
from * to last 3 sts, K2tog, yfwd, K1.
Row 2: P3, K3, *P1, P into front then back of
double yfwd of previous row, P1, K3; rep from
* to last 3 sts, P3.
Row 3: K1, K2tog, yfrn, P3, *yon, sl 1, K1,
psso, K2tog, yfrn, P3; rep from * to last 3 sts,
yon, sl 1, K1, psso, K1.
Row 4: P3, K3, *P4, K3; rep from * to last
3 sts, P3.
All sizes
These 4 rows form the pattern and are rep
throughout.
Cont in patt until back measures 60 (61: 62:
63: 64: 65) cm from cast-on edge, ending
with a WS row.
Shape shoulders and back neck
Cast off 6 (7: 7: 8: 8: 9) sts at beg of next
2 rows.
50 (52: 58: 60: 64: 68) sts.

Next row (RS): Cast off 6 (6: 7: 7: 8: 8) sts,
patt until there are 10 (10: 11: 11: 11: 12) sts
on right needle and turn, leaving rem sts on
a holder.
Work each side of neck separately.
Cast off 4 sts at beg of next row.
Cast off rem 6 (6: 7: 7: 7: 8) sts.
With RS facing rejoin yarn to rem sts, cast off
centre 18 (20: 22: 24: 26: 28) sts, patt to end.
Complete to match first side, reversing
shapings.

FRONT

Work as given for back until front measures
22 (22: 24: 24: 26: 26) cm from cast-on edge,
ending with a WS row.
Divide for front opening
Next row (RS): Patt 29 (31: 33: 35: 37: 40)
sts and slip these onto a holder for left front,
K4 (4: 6: 6: 6: 6), patt to end.
33 (35: 39: 41: 43: 46) sts.
Next row: Patt to last 4 (4: 6: 6: 6: 6) sts,
K4 (4: 6: 6: 6: 6).
Working 4 (4: 6: 6: 6: 6) sts at centre front
in garter st and rem sts in patt, cont straight
until 10 (12: 14: 16: 16: 18) rows less have
been worked than back to start of shoulder
shaping, ending with a WS row.
Shape front neck
Next row (RS): Patt 11 (11: 12: 12: 13: 13)
sts and slip these sts onto a holder, patt to end.
22 (24: 27: 29: 30: 33) sts.
Keeping patt correct, dec 1 st at neck edge of
next 2 rows, then on foll 1 (2: 3: 4: 4: 5) alt
rows, then on foll 4th row.
18 (19: 21: 22: 23: 25) sts.
Work 2 rows, ending with a **RS** row.
Shape shoulder
Cast off 6 (7: 7: 8: 8: 9) sts at beg of next
row, then 6 (6: 7: 7: 8: 8) sts at beg of foll
alt row.
Work 1 row.
Cast off rem 6 (6: 7: 7: 7: 8) sts.
With **WS** facing rejoin yarn to rem sts, cast on
4 (4: 6: 6: 6: 6) sts, patt to end.
33 (35: 39: 41: 43: 46) sts.

Next row: Patt to last 4 (4: 6: 6: 6: 6) sts, K4 (4: 6: 6: 6: 6).

Working 4 (4: 6: 6: 6: 6) sts at centre front in garter st and rem sts in patt, cont straight until 10 (12: 14: 16: 16: 18) rows less have been worked than back to start of shoulder shaping, ending with a WS row.

Shape front neck

Next row (RS): Patt to last 11 (11: 12: 12: 13: 13) sts and turn, leaving rem sts on a holder.

22 (24: 27: 29: 30: 33) sts.

Keeping patt correct, dec 1 st at neck edge of next 2 rows, then on foll 1 (2: 3: 4: 4: 5) alt rows, then on foll 4th row.

18 (19: 21: 22: 23: 25) sts.

Work 1 row, ending with a WS row.

Shape shoulder

Cast off 6 (7: 7: 8: 8: 9) sts at beg of next row, then 6 (6: 7: 7: 8: 8) sts at beg of foll alt row.

Work 1 row.

Cast off rem 6 (6: 7: 7: 7: 8) sts.

SLEEVES (both alike)

Cast on 59 (59: 63: 63: 67: 67) sts using 6mm (US 10) needles and work from chart for sleeve as folls:

Foundation row (WS): P0 (0: 2: 2: 4: 4), K3, *P4, K3; rep from * to last 0 (0: 2: 2: 4: 4) sts, P0 (0: 2: 2: 4: 4).

Cont in patt as folls:

XS and S sizes

Row 1 (RS): P3, *K2tog, (yfwd) twice, sl 1, K1, psso, P3; rep from * to end.

Row 2: K3, *P1, P into front then back of double yfwd of previous row, P1, K3; rep from * to end.

Row 3: P3, *yon, sl 1, K1, psso, K2tog, yfrn, P3; rep from * to end.

Row 4: K3, *P4, K3; rep from * to end.

M and L sizes

Row 1 (RS): K2, P3, *K2tog, (yfwd) twice, sl 1, K1, psso, P3; rep from * to last 2 sts, K2.

Row 2: P2, K3, *P1, P into front then back of double yfwd of previous row, P1, K3; rep from * to last 2 sts, P2.

Row 3: K2tog, yfrn, P3, *yon, sl 1, K1, psso, K2tog, yfrn, P3; rep from * to last 2 sts, yon, sl 1, K1, psso.

Row 4: P2, K3, *P4, K3; rep from * to last 2 sts, P2.

XL and XXL sizes

Row 1 (RS): *K2tog, (yfwd) twice, sl 1, K1, psso, P3; rep from * to last 4 sts, K2tog, (yfwd) twice, sl 1, K1, psso.

Row 2: *P1, P into front then back of double yfwd of previous row, P1, K3; rep from * to last 4 sts, P1, P into front then back of double yfwd of previous row, P1.

Row 3: K2, K2tog, yfrn, P3, *yon, sl 1, K1, psso, K2tog, yfrn, P3; rep from * to last 4 sts, yon, sl 1, K1, psso, K2.

Row 4: *P4, K3; rep from * to last 4 sts, P4.

All sizes

These 4 rows form the pattern and are rep throughout.

Cont in patt, shaping sides by inc 1 st at each end of 11th and 2 foll 14th rows, taking inc sts into patt. 65 (65: 69: 69: 73: 73) sts.

Cont straight until sleeve measures 23 (23: 24: 24: 25: 25) cm, ending with a WS row.

Cast off.

MAKING UP

Pin out the pieces and press carefully following instructions on ball band.

Join both shoulder seams using back stitch, or mattress stitch if preferred.

Collar

With RS facing and using 5 ½mm (US 9) needles, slip 11 (11: 12: 12: 13: 13) sts from right front holder onto right needle, rejoin yarn and pick up and knit 15 (17: 19: 21: 21: 23) sts up right side of neck, 23 (25: 27: 29: 31: 33) sts from back, and 15 (17: 19: 21: 21: 23) sts down left side of neck, then patt 11 (11: 12: 12: 13: 13) sts from left front holder. 75 (81: 89: 95: 99: 105) sts.

Row 1 (RS of collar, WS of body): K5 (5: 7: 7: 7: 7), P1, *K1, P1; rep from * to last 5 (5: 7: 7: 7: 7) sts, K5 (5: 7: 7: 7: 7).

Row 2: K4 (4: 6: 6: 6: 6), P1, *K1, P1; rep from * to last 4 (4: 6: 6: 6: 6) sts, K4 (4: 6: 6: 6: 6).

These 2 rows set the sts.

Cont as set for a further 6 rows.

Change to 6mm (US 10) needles.

Cont as set until collar measures 16 cm from pick-up row.

Cast off in patt.

Mark points along side seam edges 24 (24: 25: 25: 26: 26) cm either side of shoulder seams and sew sleeves to back and front between these points. Join side and sleeve seams.

At base of front opening, sew cast-on edge in place on inside. Overlap garter st borders and sew on buttons through both layers, posilioning first button 4 cm up from base of opening and rem 2 buttons each 5 cm above previous button.

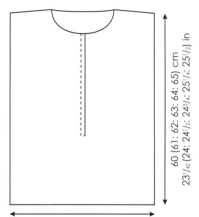

44.5 (47: 51.5: 54.5: 57: 61.5) cm
17½ (18½: 20¼: 21½: 22½: 24¼) in

60 (61: 62: 63: 64: 65) cm
23½ (24: 24½: 24¾: 25¼: 25½) in

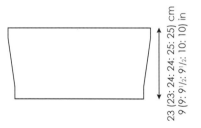

23 (23: 24: 24: 25: 25) cm
9 (9: 9½: 9½: 10: 10) in

CHARITY

CAPE WITH SINGLE HORN BUTTON

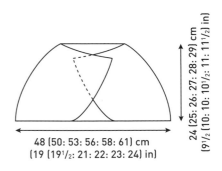

Recommendation

Suitable for the knitter with a little experience.
Please see pages 12 & 36 for photographs.

	XS	S	M	L	XL	XXL	
To fit	**81**	**86**	**91**	**97**	**102**	**107**	cm
bust	32	34	36	38	40	42	in

Rowan Big Wool

3   3   3   3   4   4   x 100gm

Photographed in Acer

Button – 1

Needles

1 pair 10mm (no 000) (US 15) needles
1 pair 12mm (US 17) needles

Tension

8 sts and 12 rows to 10 cm measured over
stocking stitch using 12mm (US 17) needles.

Special abbreviations

MP = Make picot: cast on 1 st, cast off 1 st.
(See information page for details)
Sl 2 tog = slip next 2 sts as though to K2tog.
P2sso = Pass 2 slipped sts over.

MAIN KNITTING

Cast on 64 (68: 72: 76: 78: 82) sts using
12mm (US 17) needles and work in st st as folls:
Place a marker on the 13th (14th: 15th:
16th: 16th: 17th) st in from each end to
denote the side seam.
Row 1 (RS): Knit.
Row 2 (inc): Inc 1 st at each end of next row.
66 (70: 74: 78: 80: 84) sts.
Row 3 (inc)(dec): Inc in fi rst st, (K to within
1 st of marked st, sl 2 tog, K1, p2sso) twice,
K to last st, inc in last st.
64 (68: 72: 76: 78: 82) sts.
Work 1 row.
Inc 1 st at each end of next row and 1 (1: 1:
1: 2: 2) foll alt rows.
68 (72: 76: 80: 84: 88) sts.
Work 1 row.
Next row (RS) (dec): (K to within 1 st of
marked st, sl 2 tog, K1, p2sso) twice, K
to end. 64 (68: 72: 76: 80: 84) sts.
M & L sizes only
Work 3 rows.
Next row (RS) (dec): (K to within 1 st of
marked st, sl 2 tog, K1, p2sso), K to end.
68 (72) sts.
All sizes
Work 4 (4: 2: 2: 4: 4) rows, ending with
a **RS** row.
Leave sts on a spare needle.
Right front edging (worked from side)
Cast on 7 (8: 8: 8: 9: 9) sts using 12mm (US 17)
needles.
Row 1 (RS): MP, K to end.
Row 2: Knit.
Rep these 2 rows until 41 (43: 47: 49: 49: 51)
rows have been completed, ending with
a **RS** row.
Leave sts on a holder.
Left front edging (worked from side)
Cast on 7 (8: 8: 8: 9: 9) sts using 12mm (US 17)
needles.
Row 1 (RS): Knit.
Row 2: MP, K to end.
Rep these 2 rows until 41 (43: 47: 49: 49: 51)
rows have been completed, ending with a **RS** row.

Join edgings and main knitting together

Change to 10mm (US 15) needles and cont
in garter st, i.e. knit every row, as folls:
Next row (WS): Work across left front edging
as folls; MP, K to last st, K tog last st of left
edging and first st of main knitting, K to last
st, K tog last st of main knitting and fi rst st
of right edging, K to end.
76 (82: 82: 86: 96: 100) sts.
Next row (RS) (dec): K13 (15: 15: 16: 19:
20), K2tog, K4, sl 2 tog, K1, P2sso, K4, K2tog
tbl, K20 (22: 22: 24: 28: 30), K2tog, K4, sl 2
tog, K1, P2sso, K4, K2tog tbl, K13 (15: 15:
16: 19: 20).
68 (74: 74: 78: 88: 92) sts.
Work 1 row.
Next row (RS)(buttonhole row): MP, K until
3 (3: 3: 3: 4: 4) sts on right needle, K2tog tbl,
(yon) twice, K2tog, K to end.
Next row: Knit across row, knitting into back
of loops made on previous row.
Next row (RS) (dec): K12 (14: 14: 15: 18:
19), K2tog, K3, sl 2 tog, K1, P2sso, K3, K2tog
tbl, K18 (20: 20: 22: 26: 28), K2tog, K3, sl
2 tog, K1, P2sso, K3, K2tog tbl, K12 (14: 14:
15: 18: 19).
60 (66: 66: 70: 80: 84) sts.
Work 1 row.
Next row (RS) (dec): K11 (13: 13: 14: 17:
18), K2tog, K2, sl 2 tog, K1, P2sso, K2, K2tog
tbl, K16 (18: 18: 20: 24: 26), K2tog, K2, sl 2
tog, K1, P2sso, K2, K2tog tbl, K11 (13: 13:
14: 17: 18). 52 (58: 58: 62: 72: 76) sts.

24 (25: 26: 27: 28: 29] cm
(9¹/₂ (10: 10: 10¹/₂: 11: 11¹/₂) in)

48 (50: 53: 56: 58: 61) cm
(19 (19¹/₂: 21: 22: 23: 24) in)

Continued on opposite page...

CLARA

SLIM FITTING WAISTCOAT WITH POCKET DETAIL

Recommendation
Suitable for the knitter with a little experience.
Please see pages 8 & 9 for photographs.

	XS	S	M	L	XL	XXL	
To fit	**81**	**86**	**91**	**97**	**102**	**109**	**cm**
bust	32	34	36	38	40	43	in

Rowan Classic Cashsoft 4 ply
     5   6   6   7   8   9   x 50gm
Photographed in Cherish^K
^K Kim Hargreaves for Rowan Classic

Buttons – 6

Needles
1 pair 2 ¾mm (no 12) (US 2) needles
1 pair 3mm (no 11) (US 2/3) needles

Tension
28 sts and 38 rows to 10 cm measured over
stocking stitch using 3mm (US 2/3) needles.

Left back underarm edging
Cast on 7 sts using 2 ¾mm (US 2) needles.
Row 1 (RS): K1, (P1, K1) 3 times.
Row 2: As row 1.
Rows 3 and 4: P1, (K1, P1) 3 times.
These 4 rows form double moss st.
Cont in double moss st for a further
16 (18: 18: 18: 18: 20) rows, ending
with a WS row.
Break yarn and leave sts on a holder.

Right back underarm edging
Cast on 7 sts using 2 ¾mm (US 2) needles.
Work in double moss st as given for left
back underarm edging until 19 (21: 21:
21: 21: 23) rows have been completed,
ending with a **RS** row.
Break yarn and leave sts on a holder.

BACK
Cast on 113 (121: 127: 135: 141: 153) sts
using 2 ¾mm (US 2) needles.
Work in garter st for 3 rows, ending with
a **RS** row.
Rows 4 and 5: P1 (1: 0: 0: 1: 1), *K1, P1; rep
from * to last 0 (0: 1: 1: 0: 0) st, K0 (0: 1: 1:
0: 0).
Rows 6 and 7: K1 (1: 0: 0: 1: 1), *P1, K1; rep
from * to last 0 (0: 1: 1: 0: 0) st, P0 (0: 1: 1: 0: 0).

Last 4 rows form double moss st.
Work in double moss st for a further 6 rows,
ending with a **RS** row.
Change to 3mm (US 2/3) needles.
Beg with a **purl** row, work in st st for 3 rows,
ending with a WS row.
Next row (dec) (RS): K3, K2tog, K to last
5 sts, K2tog tbl, K3.
Working all side seam decreases as set by last
row, dec 1 st at each end of 8th and 0 (0: 2:
2: 2: 2) foll 8th rows, then on 6 (6: 4: 4: 4: 4)
foll 6th rows.
97 (105: 111: 119: 125: 137) sts.
Work 21 rows, ending with a WS row.
Next row (inc) (RS): K3, M1, K to last 3 sts,
M1, K3.
Working all side seam increases as set
by last row, inc 1 st at each end of 6th
and 5 foll 8th rows.
111 (119: 125: 133: 139: 151) sts.
Work 9 rows, ending with a WS row.
(Back should measure approx 38 (38: 39:
39: 39: 39) cm.)
Shape armholes
Cast off 5 (5: 5: 6: 6: 7) sts at beg of next
2 rows. 101 (109: 115: 121: 127: 137) sts.
Dec 1 st at each end of next 9 (11: 11: 11:
11: 13) rows, ending with a **RS** row.
83 (87: 93: 99: 105: 111) sts.

Continued on next page...

Charity – Continued from previous page.

XL & XXL sizes only
Work 1 row.
Next row (RS) (dec): K16 (17), K2tog, K1, sl
2 tog, K1, P2sso, K1, K2tog tbl, K24 (26),
K2tog, K1, sl 2 tog, K1, P2sso, K1, K2tog tbl,
K16 (17).
64 (68) sts.
All sizes
Cast off knitwise (on WS).

Stitch the front edgings into place around the
front curves to side seam marker, preferably
using mattress stitch.
Lower edging for back
Cast on 7 (8: 8: 8: 9: 9) sts using 12mm
(US 17) needles.
Row 1 (RS): MP, K to end.
Row 2: Knit.
Rep these 2 rows until 64 (68: 70: 74: 78: 80)

rows have been completed, ending with a
WS row.
Cast off.
Stitch the top (straight edge) of the edging
into place between the markers across the
cast-on edge of the main knitting.
Join the front and back edgings together at
side seams.
Sew on button.

Join underarm edgings

Next row (WS): With WS facing, slip 7 sts of left back underarm edging onto right needle, slip last of these sts back onto left needle and P tog this last st of edging with first st of back, P to last st of back, P tog last st of back with first st of right back underarm edging, patt rem 6 sts of edging.
95 (99: 105: 111: 117: 123) sts.

Next row (dec) (RS): Patt 6 sts, K2tog, K to last 8 sts, K2tog tbl, patt 6 sts.

Keeping sts correct as set and working all armhole decreases as set by last row, dec 1 st at each end of 2nd and foll 4 (4: 5: 5: 6: 6) alt rows, then on 2 foll 4th rows, then on foll 6th row. 77 (81: 85: 91: 95: 101) sts.

Cont straight until armhole measures 21 (22: 22: 23: 24: 25) cm, ending with a WS row.

Shape shoulders and back neck

Cast off 6 sts at beg of next 2 rows.
65 (69: 73: 79: 83: 89) sts.

Next row (RS): Cast off 8 (8: 9: 10: 10: 11) sts, K until there are 11 (12: 12: 13: 14: 15) sts on right needle and turn, leaving rem sts on a holder.

Work each side of neck separately.

Cast off 4 sts at beg of next row.

Cast off rem 7 (8: 8: 9: 10: 11) sts.

With RS facing rejoin yarn to rem sts, cast off centre 27 (29: 31: 33: 35: 37) sts, K to end.

Complete to match first side, reversing shapings.

Pocket linings (make two)

Cast on 27 (28: 29: 29: 30: 30) sts using 3mm (US 2/3) needles.

Beg with a K row, work in st st for 30 (32: 34: 34: 36: 36) rows, ending with a WS row.

Break yarn and leave sts on a holder.

Left front underarm edging

Work as given for right back underarm edging.

LEFT FRONT

Cast on 61 (65: 68: 72: 75: 81) sts using 2 ¾mm (US 2) needles.

Work in garter st for 3 rows, ending with a **RS** row.

Row 4: P1, *K1, P1; rep from * to last 0 (0: 1: 1: 0: 0) st, K0 (0: 1: 1: 0: 0).

Row 5: P1 (1: 0: 0: 1: 1), *K1, P1; rep from * to end.

Row 6: K1, *P1, K1; rep from * to last 0 (0: 1: 1: 0: 0) st, P0 (0: 1: 1: 0: 0).

Row 7: K1 (1: 0: 0: 1: 1), *P1, K1; rep from * to end.

Last 4 rows form double moss st.

Work in double moss st for a further 6 rows, ending with a **RS** row.

Change to 3mm (US 2/3) needles.

Row 14 (WS): Patt 6 sts, K1, P to end.

Row 15: K to last 7 sts, P1, patt 6 sts.

These 2 rows set the sts.

Keeping sts correct as set, work 1 row, ending with a WS row.

Working all side seam decreases as set by back, dec 1 st at beg of next and 1 (1: 3: 3: 3: 3) foll 8th rows, then on 2 (3: 0: 0: 1: 1) foll 6th rows.
57 (60: 64: 68: 70: 76) sts.

Work 5 (1: 5: 5: 1: 1) rows, ending with a WS row.

Place pocket

Next row (RS): (K3, K2tog) 1 (0: 1: 1: 0: 0) times, K7 (13: 9: 11: 15: 18), slip next 27 (28: 29: 29: 30: 30) sts onto a holder and, in their place, K across 27 (28: 29: 29: 30: 30) sts of first pocket lining, patt 18 (19: 21: 23: 25: 28) sts.
56 (60: 63: 67: 70: 76) sts.

Dec 1 st at beg of 6th (4th: 6th: 6th: 4th: 4th) and 2 foll 6th rows.
53 (57: 60: 64: 67: 73) sts.

Work 21 rows, ending with a WS row.

Shape front slope

Next row (RS): K3, M1 (for side seam inc), K to last 9 sts, K2tog tbl (for front slope dec), patt 7 sts.

Working all side seam increases and all front slope decreases as set by last row, inc 1 st at beg of 6th and 5 foll 8th rows and **at same time** dec 1 st at front slope edge of 8th and 4 foll 8th rows.
54 (58: 61: 65: 68: 74) sts.

Work 9 rows, dec 1 st at front slope edge on 2nd of these rows and ending with a WS row.
53 (57: 60: 64: 67: 73) sts.

Shape armhole

Cast off 5 (5: 5: 6: 6: 7) sts at beg and dec 1 st at end of next row.
47 (51: 54: 57: 60: 65) sts.

Work 1 row.

Dec 1 st at armhole edge of next 9 (11: 11: 11: 11: 13) rows, ending with a **RS** row, and **at same time** dec 1 st at front slope edge of 7th row.
37 (39: 42: 45: 48: 51) sts.

Join underarm edging

Next row (WS): Patt to last st of left front, P tog last st of left front with first st of left front underarm edging, patt rem 6 sts of edging.
43 (45: 48: 51: 54: 57) sts.

Keeping sts correct as set and working all armhole decreases as set by back, dec 1 st at armhole edge of next and foll 5 (5: 6: 6: 7: 7) alt rows, then on 2 foll 4th rows, then on foll 6th row and at same time dec 1 st at front slope edge of 5th (3rd: 3rd: 3rd: 3rd: next) and 2 (2: 3: 3: 3: 3) foll 8th rows. 31 (33: 34: 37: 39: 42) sts.

Dec 1 st at front slope edge **only** on 4th (2nd: 6th: 6th: 4th: 2nd) and 1 (2: 0: 0: 0: 0) foll 8th rows, then on 1 (1: 3: 4: 5: 6) foll 6th rows. 28 (29: 30: 32: 33: 35) sts.

Cont straight until left front matches back to beg of shoulder shaping, ending with a WS row.

Shape shoulder

Cast off 6 sts at beg of next row, 8 (8: 9: 10: 10: 11) sts at beg of foll alt row, then 7 (8: 8: 9: 10: 11) sts at beg of foll alt row. 7 sts.

Cont in patt on these 7 sts only for back neck border extension for a further 6 (6.5: 6.5: 7: 7.5: 8) cm, ending with a WS row.

Cast off.

Mark positions for 6 buttons along left front opening edge – first to come in row 7, last button to come just below beg of front slope shaping, and rem 4 buttons evenly spaced between.

Right front underarm edging

Work as given for left back underarm edging.

RIGHT FRONT

Cast on 61 (65: 68: 72: 75: 81) sts using 2 ¾mm (US 2) needles.

Work in garter st for 3 rows, ending with a **RS** row.

Row 4: P1 (1: 0: 0: 1: 1), *K1, P1; rep from * to end.

Row 5: P1, *K1, P1; rep from * to last 0 (0: 1: 1: 0: 0) st, K0 (0: 1: 1: 0: 0).

Row 6: K1 (1: 0: 0: 1: 1), *P1, K1; rep from * to end.

Last 3 rows set position of double moss st as given for back.

Keeping double moss st correct as now set, cont as follows:

Row 7 (buttonhole row) (RS): Patt, work 2 tog, yrn (to make a buttonhole), patt to end.

Working a further 5 buttonholes in this way to correspond to positions marked for buttons on left front and noting that no further reference will be made to buttonholes, cont as follows:

Work in double moss st for a further 6 rows, ending with a **RS** row.

Change to 3mm (US 2/3) needles.

Row 14 (WS): P to last 7 sts, K1, patt 6 sts.

Row 15: Patt 6 sts, P1, K to end.

These 2 rows set the sts.

Keeping sts correct as set, work 1 row, ending with a WS row.

Working all side seam decreases as set by back, dec 1 st at end of next and 1 (1: 3: 3: 3: 3) foll 8th rows, then on 2 (3: 0: 0: 1: 1) foll 6th rows.

57 (60: 64: 68: 70: 76) sts.

Work 5 (1: 5: 5: 1: 1) rows, ending with a WS row.

Place pocket

Next row (RS): Patt 18 (19: 21: 23: 25: 28) sts, slip next 27 (28: 29: 29: 30: 30) sts onto a holder and, in their place, K across 27 (28: 29: 29: 30: 30) sts of second pocket lining, K7 (13: 9: 11: 15: 18), (K2tog tbl, K3) 1 (0: 1: 1: 0: 0) times. 56 (60: 63: 67: 70: 76) sts.

Dec 1 st at end of 6th (4th: 6th: 6th: 4th: 4th) and 2 foll 6th rows.

53 (57: 60: 64: 67: 73) sts.

Work 21 rows, ending with a WS row.

Shape front slope

Next row (RS): Patt 7 sts, K2tog (for front slope dec), K to last 3 sts, M1 (for side seam inc), K3.

Working all side seam increases and all front slope decreases as set by last row, complete to match left front, reversing shapings.

MAKING UP

Pin out the pieces and press carefully following instructions on ball band.

Join both shoulder seams using back stitch, or mattress stitch if preferred. Join cast-off ends of back neck border extensions, then neatly slip stitch row-end edge in place to back neck edge.

Pocket tops (both alike)

Slip 27 (28: 29: 29: 30: 30) sts from pocket holder onto 2 ¾mm (US 2) needles and rejoin yarn with RS facing.

Beg with a K row, work in st st for 6 rows, ending with a WS row.

Cast off.

Sew side seams. Join cast-on edges of underarm edgings, then neatly slip stitch in place.

Sew pocket linings in place on inside. Allow pocket tops to roll to RS, then neatly sew in place as in photograph.

Sew on buttons.

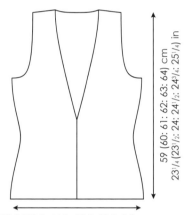

39.5 (42.5: 44.5: 47.5: 49.5: 54) cm
15¹/₂ (16³/₄: 17¹/₂: 18³/₄: 19¹/₂: 21¹/₄) in

59 (60: 61: 62: 63: 64) cm
23¹/₄ (23¹/₂: 24: 24¹/₂: 24³/₄: 25¹/₄) in

OCTAVIA

BELTED JACKET WITH TEXTURED SHAWL COLLAR

Recommendation

Suitable for the knitter with a little experience.
Please see pages 10 & 11 for photographs.

	XS	S	M	L	XL	XXL	
To fit	**81**	**86**	**91**	**97**	**101**	**109**	**cm**
bust	32	34	36	38	40	43	in

Rowan Cocoon

8   9   10   11   12   13 x 100gm
Photographed in Seascape

Needles

1 pair 6mm (no 4) (US 10) needles
1 pair 6 ½mm (no 3) (US 10 ½) needles
1 pair 7mm (no 2) (US 10 ½/11) needles

Tension

14 sts and 17 rows to 10 cm measured over
stocking stitch using 7mm (US 10 ½/11)
needles.

BACK

Cast on 59 (63: 67: 71: 75: 81) sts using
6 ½mm (US 10 ½) needles.
Rows 1 and 2: P1 (1: 1: 1: 1: 0), *K1, P1; rep
from * to last 0 (0: 0: 0: 0: 1) st, K0 (0: 0: 0: 0: 0: 1).
Rows 3 and 4: K1 (1: 1: 1: 1: 0), *P1, K1; rep
from * to last 0 (0: 0: 0: 0: 1) st, P0 (0: 0: 0:
0: 1).
These 4 rows form double moss st.
Work in double moss st for 4 rows more,
ending with a WS row.
Change to 7mm (US 10 ½/11) needles.
Beg with a K row, work in st st for 2 rows.
Next row (dec) (RS): K2, K2tog, K to last
4 sts, K2tog tbl, K2.
Working all side seam decreases as set by
last row, cont in st st, dec 1 st at each end
of 8th and foll 8th row, then on foll 6th row.
51 (55: 59: 63: 67: 73) sts.
Work 11 rows, ending with a WS row.
Next row (inc) (RS): K2, M1, K to last 2 sts,
M1, K2.
Working all side seam increases as set by
last row, inc 1 st at each end of 8th and
2 foll 8th rows.
59 (63: 67: 71: 75: 81) sts.
Work 5 (5: 7: 7: 7: 7) rows, ending with a WS row.
(Back should measure approx 43 (43: 44: 44:
44: 44) cm.)
Shape armholes
Cast off 3 (3: 3: 3: 3: 4) sts at beg of next 2
rows. 53 (57: 61: 65: 69: 73) sts.
Dec 1 st at each end of next 3 rows, then on
foll 1 (2: 3: 3: 4: 5) alt rows, then on
foll 4th row. 43 (45: 47: 51: 53: 55) sts.
Cont straight until armhole measures 18 (19:
19: 20: 21: 22) cm, ending with a WS row.
Shape shoulders and back neck
Cast off 4 (4: 4: 5: 5: 5) sts at beg of next 2
rows. 35 (37: 39: 41: 43: 45) sts.
Next row (RS): Cast off 4 (4: 4: 5: 5: 5) sts,
K until there are 8 (8: 8: 8: 8: 9) sts on right
needle and turn, leaving rem sts on a holder.
Work each side of neck separately.
Cast off 4 sts at beg of next row.
Cast off rem 4 (4: 4: 4: 4: 5) sts.

With RS facing rejoin yarn to rem sts, cast off
centre 11 (13: 15: 15: 17: 17) sts, K to end.
Complete to match first side, reversing shapings.

LEFT FRONT

Cast on 38 (40: 42: 44: 46: 49) sts using
6 ½mm (US 10 ½) needles.
Row 1 (RS): P1 (1: 1: 1: 1: 0), *K1, P1; rep
from * to last st, K1.
Row 2: *K1, P1; rep from * to last 0 (0: 0:
0: 0: 1) st, K0 (0: 0: 0: 0: 0: 1).
Row 3: K1 (1: 1: 1: 1: 0), *P1, K1; rep from *
to last st, P1.
Row 4: *P1, K1; rep from * to last 0 (0: 0:
0: 0: 1) st, P0 (0: 0: 0: 0: 0: 1).
These 4 rows form double moss st.
Work in double moss st for 4 rows more,
ending with a WS row.
Change to 7mm (US 10 ½/11) needles.
Row 9 (RS): K to last 6 sts, patt 6 sts.
Row 10: Patt 6 sts, P to end.
These 2 rows set the sts – front opening edge
6 sts still in double moss st with all other sts
now worked in st st.
Keeping sts correct as set and working all side
seam decreases as set by back, dec 1 st at beg
of next and 2 foll 8th rows, then on foll 6th row.
34 (36: 38: 40: 42: 45) sts.
Work 7 rows, ending with a WS row.
Shape front slope
Dec 1 st at end of next and foll 4 (6: 7: 7: 8: 8)
alt rows, then on 6 (5: 5: 5: 4: 4) foll 4th rows and
at same time, working all side seam increases
as set by back, inc 1 st at beg of next and 3 foll
8th rows. 27 (28: 29: 31: 33: 36) sts.
Work 1 (1: 1: 1: 2: 2) rows, ending with a WS row.
Shape armhole
Cast off 3 (3: 3: 3: 3: 4) sts at beg and dec
0 (0: 0: 0: 1: 1) st at end of next row.
24 (25: 26: 28: 29: 31) sts. Work 1 row.
Dec 1 st at armhole edge of next 3 rows, then
on foll 1 (2: 3: 3: 4: 5) alt rows, then on foll
4th row and **at same time** dec 1 st at front
slope edge on next (next: next: next: 3rd: 3rd)
and 2 (2: 3: 3: 3: 3) foll 4th rows.
16 (16: 15: 17: 17: 18) sts.

Dec 1 st at front slope edge **only** on 4th (2nd: 4th: 4th: 4th: 2nd) and 3 (3: 2: 2: 2: 2) foll 4th rows. 12 (12: 12: 14: 14: 15) sts.
Cont straight until left front matches back to beg of shoulder shaping, ending with a WS row.

Shape shoulder
Cast off 4 (4: 4: 5: 5: 5) sts at beg of next and foll alt row.
Work 1 row. Cast off rem 4 (4: 4: 4: 4: 5) sts.

RIGHT FRONT
Cast on 38 (40: 42: 44: 46: 49) sts using 6 ½mm (US 10 ½) needles.
Row 1 (RS): *K1, P1; rep from * to last 0 (0: 0: 0: 0: 1) st, K0 (0: 0: 0: 0: 1).
Row 2: P1 (1: 1: 1: 1: 0), *K1, P1; rep from * to last st, K1.
Row 3: *P1, K1; rep from * to last 0 (0: 0: 0: 0: 1) st, P0 (0: 0: 0: 0: 1).
Row 4: K1 (1: 1: 1: 1: 0), *P1, K1; rep from * to last st, P1.
These 4 rows form double moss st.
Work in double moss st for 4 rows more, ending with a WS row.
Change to 7mm (US 10 ½/11) needles.
Row 9 (RS): Patt 6 sts, K to end.
Row 10: P to last 6 sts, patt 6 sts.
These 2 rows set the sts – front opening edge 6 sts still in double moss st with all other sts now worked in st st.
Keeping sts correct as set and working all side seam decreases as set by back, dec 1 st at end of next and 2 foll 8th rows, then on foll 6th row. 34 (36: 38: 40: 42: 45) sts.
Complete to match left front, reversing shapings.

SLEEVES (both alike)
Cast on 61 (63: 65: 65: 67: 69) sts using 7mm (US 10 ½/11) needles.
Beg with a K row, work in st st, shaping sides by dec 1 st at each end of 5th and 4 foll 4th rows, then on 2 foll 6th rows, then on foll 8th row, then on foll 10th row. 43 (45: 47: 47: 49: 51) sts.
Cont straight until sleeve measures 41 (42: 44: 45: 46: 46) cm, ending with a WS row.

Shape top
Cast off 3 (3: 3: 3: 3: 4) sts at beg of next 2 rows. 37 (39: 41: 41: 43: 43) sts.
Dec 1 st at each end of next and foll 3 (3: 3: 2: 2: 2) alt rows, then on 2 (2: 2: 3: 3: 4) foll 4th rows, then on foll 2 (2: 2: 2: 3: 2) alt rows, then on foll 3 rows, end with a WS row.
Cast off rem 15 (17: 19: 19: 19: 19) sts.

Cuffs (both alike)
With RS facing and using 6mm (US 10) needles, pick up and knit 61 (63: 65: 65: 67: 69) sts from cast-on edge of sleeve.
Row 1 (WS): P0 (0: 0: 2: 1: 0), (P2tog) 14 (13: 12: 31: 33: 16) times, (P3tog) 1 (3: 5: 0: 0: 1) times, (P2tog) 15 (14: 13: 0: 0: 17) times, P0 (0: 0: 1: 0: 0).
30 (30: 30: 34: 34: 34) sts.
Row 2: K2, *P2, K2; rep from * to end.
Row 3: P2, *K2, P2; rep from * to end.
Rep last 2 rows until cuff measures 10 cm from pick-up row.
Cast off in rib.

MAKING UP
Pin out the pieces and press carefully following instructions on ball band.
Join both shoulder seams using back stitch, or mattress stitch if preferred.

Collar
Cast on 113 (117: 121: 125: 129: 133) sts using 6 ½mm (US 10 ½) needles.
Row 1 (RS): Purl.
Now work in patt as follows:
Row 1 (WS): Purl.
Row 2: P1, *(K1, yfwd, K1, yfwd, K1) all into next st, P1; rep from * to end.
Row 3: Knit.
Row 4: P1, *K5tog, P1; rep from * to end.
Row 5: P2tog, P to last 2 sts, P2tog.
111 (115: 119: 123: 127: 131) sts.
Rows 6 to 8: As rows 2 to 4.
These 8 rows form patt and beg collar shaping.
Keeping patt correct, dec 1 st at each end of next and foll 5 alt rows, ending with a WS row.
99 (103: 107: 111: 115: 119) sts.
Cast off 2 sts at beg of next 8 rows, then 3 sts at beg of foll 14 (14: 14: 16: 16: 16) rows, then – (-: -: 4: 4: 4) sts at beg of next – (-: -: 2: 2: 2) rows.
Cast off rem 41 (45: 49: 39: 43: 47) sts.
Matching ends of collar cast-on edge to beg of front slope shaping, sew shaped row-end and cast-off edges of collar to neck edges.
Join side seams. Join sleeve and cuff seams.
Set in sleeves.

Belt
Cast on 1 st using 6mm (US 10) needles.
Row 1 (RS): Inc in st. 2 sts.
Row 2: P1, K1.
Row 3: Inc in first st, K1. 3 sts.

Row 4: K1, P1, K1.
Row 5: Inc in first st, K1, P1. 4 sts.
Row 6: (P1, K1) twice.
Row 7: Inc in first st, K1, P1, K1. 5 sts.
Row 8: (K1, P1) twice, K1.
Row 9: Inc in first st, (K1, P1) twice. 6 sts.
Row 10: (P1, K1) 3 times.
Row 11: Inc in first st, (K1, P1) twice, K1. 7 sts.
Row 12: (K1, P1) 3 times, K1.
These 12 rows set position of double moss st and complete shaping.
Cont in double moss st until belt measures 115 (120: 125: 130: 135: 145) cm from cast-on edge, ending with a WS row.
Dec 1 st at end of next and foll 5 alt rows.
Cast off rem 1 st.
Try on garment and mark waist position.
Make belt loops (by working a short length of crochet chain or by finger knitting) on side seams at waist position and thread belt through loops.

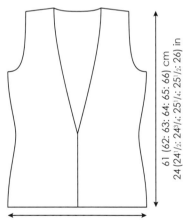

42 (45: 48: 50.5: 53.5: 58) cm
16½ (17¾: 19: 20: 21: 22¾) in

61 (62: 63: 64: 65: 66) cm
24 (24½: 24¾: 25¼: 25½: 26) in

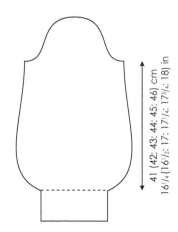

41 (42: 43: 44: 45: 46) cm
16¼ (16½: 17: 17¼: 17¾: 18) in

NELL

BELTED CABLED CARDIGAN

Pattern note: When casting off across top of cables, work K2tog twice (or 3 times, depending on width of cable) to reduce the number of sts in seam. The number of sts stated in patt relates to the actual number of sts cast off.

BACK

Cast on 92 (96: 100: 102: 104: 112) sts using 6 ½mm (US 10 ½) needles.

Row 1 (RS): K0 (0: 1: 0: 0: 1), P1 (1: 2: 0: 1: 2), (K2, P2) 3 (3: 3: 4: 4: 4) times, K4, P2, K2, P2, K6, P2, K2, P2, K4, P2, (K2, P2) 3 (4: 4: 4: 4: 5) times, K4, P2, K2, P2, K6, P2, K2, P2, K4, (P2, K2) 3 (3: 3: 4: 4: 4) times, P1 (1: 2: 0: 1: 2), K0 (0: 1: 0: 0: 1).

Row 2: P0 (0: 1: 0: 0: 1), K1 (1: 2: 0: 1: 2), (P2, K2) 3 (3: 3: 4: 4: 4) times, P4, K2, P2, K2, P6, K2, P2, K2, P4, K2, (P2, K2) 3 (4: 4: 4: 4: 5) times, P4, K2, P2, K2, P6, K2, P2, K2, P4, (K2, P2) 3 (3: 3: 4: 4: 4) times, K1 (1: 2: 0: 1: 2), P0 (0: 1: 0: 0: 1).

Rows 3 and 4: As rows 1 and 2.

Row 5: K0 (0: 1: 0: 0: 1), P1 (1: 2: 0: 1: 2), (K2, P2) 3 (3: 3: 4: 4: 4) times, C4B, P2, K2, P2, C6B, P2, K2, P2, C4B, P2, (K2, P2) 3 (4: 4: 4: 4: 5) times, C4F, P2, K2, P2, C6F, P2, K2, P2, C4F, (P2, K2) 3 (3: 3: 4: 4: 4) times, P1 (1: 2: 0: 1: 2), K0 (0: 1: 0: 0: 1).

Row 6: As row 2.

Now rep rows 1 and 2, 3 times more, dec (dec: dec: dec: inc: dec) 1 st at centre of last row and ending with a WS row.
91 (95: 99: 101: 105: 111) sts.
Change to 7mm (US 10 ½ /11) needles.
Now work in patt, placing cable panels as folls:

Row 1 (RS): P1 (1: 1: 0: 1: 1), (K1 tbl, P1) 6 (6: 7: 8: 8: 9) times, work next 26 sts as row 1 of chart A, P1, (K1 tbl, P1) 6 (8: 8: 8: 9: 10) times, work next 26 sts as row 1 of chart B, (P1, K1 tbl) 6 (6: 7: 8: 8: 9) times, P1 (1: 1: 0: 1: 1).

Row 2: K13 (13: 15: 16: 17: 19), work next 26 sts as row 2 of chart B, K13 (17: 17: 17: 19: 21), work next 26 sts as row 2 of chart A, K13 (13: 15: 16: 17: 19).

These 2 rows set the sts – 2 cable panels with textured patt between and at sides.
Cont as set, dec 1 st at each end of 15th and 3 foll 8th rows.
83 (87: 91: 93: 97: 103) sts.
Work 17 rows, ending with a WS row.
Inc 1 st at each end of next and 3 foll 8th rows, taking inc sts into patt.
91 (95: 99: 101: 105: 111) sts.
Work 7 (7: 9: 9: 13: 13) rows, ending with a WS row.

Shape armholes

Keeping patt correct, cast off 4 (4: 4: 4: 4: 5) sts at beg of next 2 rows.
83 (87: 91: 93: 97: 101) sts.
Dec 1 st at each end of next 5 (5: 5: 5: 7: 7) rows, then on foll 2 (3: 4: 4: 3: 4) alt rows.
69 (71: 73: 75: 77: 79) sts.
Cont straight until armhole measures 20 (21: 21: 22: 22: 23) cm, ending with a WS row.

Shape shoulders and back neck

Cast off 8 (7: 8: 9: 9: 9) sts at beg of next 2 rows.
53 (57: 57: 57: 59: 61) sts.

Next row (RS): Cast off 8 sts, patt until there are 13 sts on right needle and turn, leaving rem sts on a holder.
Work each side of neck separately.
Cast off 5 sts at beg of next row.
Cast off rem 8 sts.
With RS facing rejoin yarn to rem sts, cast off centre 11 (15: 15: 15: 17: 19) sts, patt to end. Complete to match first side, reversing shapings.

LEFT FRONT

Cast on 53 (54: 56: 57: 59: 61) sts using 6 ½mm (US 10 ½) needles.

Row 1 (RS): K0 (0: 1: 0: 0: 1), P1 (1: 2: 0: 1: 2), (K2, P2) 3 (3: 3: 4: 4: 4) times, K4, P2, K2, P2, K6, P2, K2, P2, K4, P2, K2, P1, K9 (10: 10: 10: 11: 11).

Row 2: K10 (11: 11: 11: 12: 12), P2, K2, P4, K2, P2, K2, P6, K2, P2, K2, P4, (K2, P2) 3 (3: 3: 4: 4: 4) times, K1 (1: 2: 0: 1: 2), P0 (0: 1: 0: 0: 1).

Rows 3 and 4: As rows 1 and 2.

Recommendation

Suitable for the knitter with a little experience.
Please see pages 14, 18 & 21 for photographs.

	XS	S	M	L	XL	XXL	
To fit	**81**	**86**	**91**	**97**	**102**	**109**	**cm**
bust	32	34	36	38	40	43	in

Rowan Classic Cashsoft Chunky

26	28	31	34	37	40	x 50 gm

Photographed in Rocky[K]
[K] Kim Hargreaves for Rowan classic

Buttons – 5

Needles

1 pair 6 ½mm (no 3) (US 10 ½) needles
1 pair 7mm (no 2) (US 10 ½ /11) needles
Cable needle

Tension

13 sts and 18 rows to 10 cm measured over stocking stitch using 7mm (US 10 ½ /11mm) needles.

Special abbreviations

cn = cable needle; **C4B** = slip next 2 sts onto cn and leave at back of work, K2, then K2 from cn; **C4F** = slip next 2 sts onto cn and leave at front of work, K2, then K2 from cn; **Cr4R** = slip next st onto cn and leave at back of work, K3, then P1 from cn; **Cr4L** = slip next 3 sts onto cn and leave at front of work, P1, then K3 from cn; **C6B** = slip next 3 sts onto cn and leave at back of work, K3, then K3 from cn; **C6F** = slip next 3 sts onto cn and leave at front of work, K3, then K3 from cn.

Row 5: K0 (0: 1: 0: 0: 1), P1 (1: 2: 0: 1: 2), (K2, P2) 3 (3: 3: 4: 4: 4) times, C4B, P2, K2, P2, C6B, P2, K2, P2, C4B, P2, K2, P1, K9 (10: 10: 10: 11: 11).

Row 6: As row 2.

Rows 7 to 12: As rows 1 and 2, 3 times.

Change to 7mm (US 10 ½ /11) needles.

Now work in patt, placing cable panel as folls:

Row 1 (RS): P1 (1: 1: 0: 1: 1), (K1 tbl, P1) 6 (6: 7: 8: 8: 9) times, work next 26 sts as row 1 of chart A, P1, (K1 tbl, P1) twice, K9 (10: 10: 10: 11: 11).

Row 2: K14 (15: 15: 15: 16: 16), work next 26 sts as row 2 of chart A, K13 (13: 15: 16: 17: 19).

These 2 rows set the sts – cable panel with textured patt either side and front opening edge in garter st.

Cont as set, dec 1 st at beg of 15th and 3 foll 8th rows. 49 (50: 52: 53: 55: 57) sts.

Work 17 rows, ending with a WS row.

Inc 1 st at beg of next and 3 foll 8th rows, taking inc sts into patt.

53 (54: 56: 57: 59: 61) sts.

Work 7 (7: 9: 9: 13: 13) rows, ending with a WS row.

Shape armhole

Keeping patt correct, cast off 4 (4: 4: 4: 4: 5) sts at beg of next row. 49 (50: 52: 53: 55: 56) sts.

Work 1 row.

Dec 1 st at armhole edge of next 5 (5: 5: 5: 7: 7) rows, then on foll 2 (3: 4: 4: 3: 4) alt rows. 42 (42: 43: 44: 45: 45) sts.

Cont straight until left front matches back to beg of shoulder shaping, ending with a WS row.**

Shape shoulder

Cast off 8 (7: 8: 9: 9: 9) sts at beg of next row, then 8 sts at beg of foll 2 alt rows. 18 (19: 19: 19: 20: 20) sts.

Work 1 row, ending with a WS row.

Break yarn and leave sts on a holder.

RIGHT FRONT

Cast on 53 (54: 56: 57: 59: 61) sts using 6 ½mm (US 10 ½) needles.

Row 1 (RS): K9 (10: 10: 10: 11: 11), P1, K2, P2, K4, P2, K2, P2, K6, P2, K2, P2, K4, (P2, K2) 3 (3: 3: 4: 4: 4) times, P1 (1: 2: 0: 1: 2), K0 (0: 1: 0: 0: 1).

Row 2: P0 (0: 1: 0: 0: 1), K1 (1: 2: 0: 1: 2), (P2, K2) 3 (3: 3: 4: 4: 4) times, P4, K2, P2, K2, P6, K2, P2, K2, P4, K2, P2, K10 (11: 11: 11: 12: 12).

Rows 3 and 4: As rows 1 and 2.

Row 5: K9 (10: 10: 10: 11: 11), P1, K2, P2, C4F, P2, K2, P2, C6F, P2, K2, P2, C4F, (P2, K2) 3 (3: 3: 4: 4: 4) times, P1 (1: 2: 0: 1: 2), K0 (0: 1: 0: 0: 1).

Row 6: As row 2.

Rows 7 to 12: As rows 1 and 2, 3 times.

Change to 7mm (US 10 ½ /11) needles.

Now work in patt, placing cable panel as folls:

Row 1 (RS): K9 (10: 10: 10: 11: 11), P1, (K1 tbl, P1) twice, work next 26 sts as row 1 of chart B, (P1, K1 tbl) 6 (6: 7: 8: 8: 9) times, P1 (1: 1: 0: 1: 1).

Row 2: K13 (13: 15: 16: 17: 19), work next 26 sts as row 2 of chart B, K14 (15: 15: 15: 16: 16).

These 2 rows set the sts – cable panel with

textured patt either side and front opening edge in garter st.

Cont as set for a further 10 rows, ending with a WS row.

Next row (buttonhole row) (RS): K3 (3: 3: 3: 4: 4), K2tog tbl, (yfwd) twice, K2tog (to make a buttonhole – on next row K into back of each yfwd of previous row), patt to end.

Making a further 5 buttonholes in this way on every foll 20th row and noting that no further reference will be made to buttonholes, cont as folls:

Cont in patt, dec 1 st at end of 4th and 3 foll 8th rows. 49 (50: 52: 53: 55: 57) sts.

Complete to match left front to **, reversing shapings.

Work 1 row, ending with a **RS** row.

Shape shoulder

Cast off 8 (7: 8: 9: 9: 9) sts at beg of next row, then 8 sts at beg of foll 2 alt rows, ending with a WS row. 18 (19: 19: 19: 20: 20) sts.

Leave sts on a holder. Do NOT break off yarn but set this ball of yarn to one side for collar.

LEFT SLEEVE

Cast on 46 (48: 50: 50: 52: 54) sts using 6 ½mm (US 10 ½) needles.

Row 1 (RS): K0 (1: 0: 0: 0: 0), P2 (2: 0: 0: 1: 2), (K2, P2) 2 (2: 3: 3: 3: 3) times, K4, P2, K2, P2, K6, P2, K2, P2, K4, (P2, K2) 2 (2: 3: 3: 3: 3) times, P2 (2: 0: 0: 1: 2), K0 (1: 0: 0: 0: 0).

Row 2: P0 (1: 0: 0: 0: 0), K2 (2: 0: 0: 1: 2), (P2, K2) 2 (2: 3: 3: 3: 3) times, P4, K2, P2, K2, P6, K2, P2, K2, P4, (K2, P2) 2 (2: 3: 3: 3: 3) times, K2 (2: 0: 0: 1: 2), P0 (1: 0: 0: 0: 0).

Key

☐	K on RS, P on WS
⊡	P on RS, K on WS
⟋	C4B
⟍	C4F
⟋▢▢⟍	Cr4R
⟍▢▢⟋	Cr4L
⟋	C6B
⟍	C6F

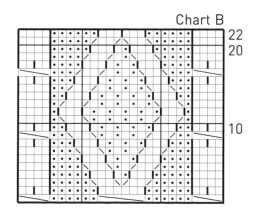

Chart B

22
20

10

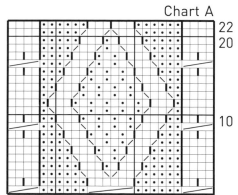

Chart A

22
20

10

Rows 3 and 4: As rows 1 and 2.
Row 5: K0 (1: 0: 0: 0: 0), P2 (2: 0: 0: 1: 2), (K2, P2) 2 (2: 3: 3: 3: 3) times, C4F, P2, K2, P2, C6F, P2, K2, P2, C4F, (P2, K2) 2 (2: 3: 3: 3: 3) times, P2 (2: 0: 0: 1: 2), K0 (1: 0: 0: 0: 0).
Row 6: As row 2.
Rows 7 to 12: As rows 1 and 2, 3 times.
Change to 7mm (US 10 ½ /11) needles.
Now work in patt, placing cable panel as folls:
Row 1 (RS): P0 (1: 0: 0: 1: 0), (K1 tbl, P1) 5 (5: 5: 6: 6: 6: 7) times, work next 26 sts as row 1 of chart B, (P1, K1 tbl) 5 (5: 6: 6: 6: 7) times, P0 (1: 0: 0: 1: 0).
Row 2: K10 (11: 12: 12: 13: 14), work next 26 sts as row 2 of chart B, K10 (11: 12: 12: 13: 14).
These 2 rows set the sts – cable panel with textured patt at sides.***
Cont as set, inc 1 st at each end of 5th and 4 foll 16th rows, taking inc sts into patt.
56 (58: 60: 60: 62: 64) sts.
Work 5 (7: 9: 11: 13: 15) rows, ending with a WS row.

Shape top
Keeping patt correct, cast off 4 (4: 4: 4: 4: 5) sts at beg of next 2 rows.
48 (50: 52: 52: 54: 54) sts.
Dec 1 st at each end of next and foll 1 (0: 0: 0: 0: 0) alt row, then on 3 (3: 3: 4: 4: 5) foll 4th rows, then on foll 2 (4: 4: 3: 4: 3) alt rows, then on foll 5 rows, ending with a WS row.
Cast off rem 24 (24: 26: 26: 26: 26) sts.

RIGHT SLEEVE
Cast on 46 (48: 50: 50: 52: 54) sts using 6 ½mm (US 10 ½) needles.
Row 1 (RS): K0 (1: 0: 0: 0: 0), P2 (2: 0: 0: 1: 2), (K2, P2) 2 (2: 3: 3: 3: 3) times, K4, P2, K2, P2, K6, P2, K2, P2, K4, (P2, K2) 2 (2: 3: 3: 3: 3) times, P2 (2: 0: 0: 1: 2), K0 (1: 0: 0: 0: 0).
Row 2: P0 (1: 0: 0: 0: 0), K2 (2: 0: 0: 1: 2), (P2, K2) 2 (2: 3: 3: 3: 3) times, P4, K2, P2, K2, P6, K2, P2, K2, P4, (K2, P2) 2 (2: 3: 3: 3: 3) times, K2 (2: 0: 0: 1: 2), P0 (1: 0: 0: 0: 0).
Rows 3 and 4: As rows 1 and 2.
Row 5: K0 (1: 0: 0: 0: 0), P2 (2: 0: 0: 1: 2), (K2, P2) 2 (2: 3: 3: 3: 3) times, C4B, P2, K2, P2, C6B, P2, K2, P2, C4B, (P2, K2) 2 (2: 3: 3: 3: 3) times, P2 (2: 0: 0: 1: 2), K0 (1: 0: 0: 0: 0).

Row 6: As row 2.
Rows 7 to 12: As rows 1 and 2, 3 times.
Change to 7mm (US 10 ½ /11) needles.
Now work in patt, placing cable panel as folls:
Row 1 (RS): P0 (1: 0: 0: 1: 0), (K1 tbl, P1) 5 (5: 6: 6: 6: 7) times, work next 26 sts as row 1 of chart A, (P1, K1 tbl) 5 (5: 6: 6: 6: 7) times, P0 (1: 0: 0: 1: 0).
Row 2: K10 (11: 12: 12: 13: 14), work next 26 sts as row 2 of chart A, K10 (11: 12: 12: 13: 14).
These 2 rows set the sts – cable panel with textured patt at sides.
Complete as given for left sleeve from ***.

MAKING UP
Pin out the pieces and press carefully following instructions on ball band.
Join both shoulder seams using back stitch, or mattress stitch if preferred.

Collar
Using ball of yarn set to one side with right front and 6 ½mm (US 10 ½) needles, work across 18 (19: 19: 19: 20: 20) sts on right front holder as folls:
K9 (10: 10: 10: 11: 11), (P2, inc in next st) 3 times, pick up and knit 23 (26: 26: 26: 29: 29) sts from back, then work across 18 (19: 19: 19: 20: 20) sts on
left front holder as folls: inc in next st, P2) 3 times, K9 (10: 10: 10: 11: 11).
65 (70: 70: 70: 75: 75) sts.
Row 1 (RS of collar, WS of body): K9 (10: 10: 10: 11: 11), (K2, P2) 3 times, K2, (inc purlwise in next st, K2) 7 (8: 8: 8: 9: 9) times, (P2, K2) 3 times, K9 (10: 10: 10: 11: 11).
72 (78: 78: 78: 84: 84) sts.
Row 2: K9 (10: 10: 10: 11: 11), (P2, K2) 13 (14: 14: 14: 15: 15) times, P2, K9 (10: 10: 10: 11: 11).
Row 3: K9 (10: 10: 10: 11: 11), (K2, P2) 13 (14: 14: 14: 15: 15) times, K11 (12: 12: 12: 13: 13).
Last 2 rows set the sts.
Cont as set for a further 7 rows.
Change to 7mm (US 10 ½ /11) needles.
Cont as set until collar measures 15 (15: 16: 16: 17: 17) cm, ending with RS of body (WS of collar) facing for next row.
Cast off in patt.
Join side seams. Join sleeve seams.
Set in sleeves. Sew on buttons.

Belt
Cast on 8 sts using 6 ½mm (US 10 ½) needles.
Work in garter st (knit every row) until belt measures 120 (120: 130: 130: 140: 140) cm.
Cast off.
Try on garment and mark waist position.
Make belt loops (by working a short length of crochet chain or by finger knitting) on side seams at waist position and thread belt through loops.

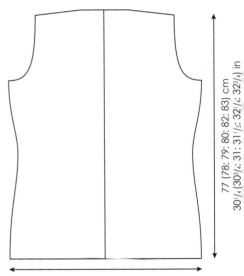

77 (78: 79: 80: 82: 83) cm
30¼ (30¾: 31: 31½: 32½: 32¾) in

59.5 (62.5: 65.5: 67: 70: 74.5) cm
23½ (24½: 25¾: 26½: 27½: 29¼) in

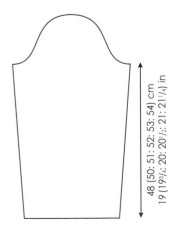

48 (50: 51: 52: 53: 54) cm
19 (19¾: 20: 20½: 21: 21¼) in

JEWEL

Recommendation

Suitable for the knitter with a little experience.
Please see pages 24 & 27 for photographs.

	XS	S	M	L	XL	XXL	
To fit	**81**	**86**	**91**	**97**	**102**	**109**	**cm**
bust	32	34	36	38	40	43	in

Rowan Classic Bamboo Soft
Three quarter length sleeve

| | 11 | 11 | 12 | 13 | 14 | 15 | x 50gm |

Angel wing sleeve

| | 10 | 10 | 11 | 12 | 13 | 14 | x 50gm |

Photographed in Jewel ᴷ / Diva ᴷ
ᴷ Kim Hargreaves for Rowan Classic

Buttons – 3 or 3 frames

Needles

1 pair 3mm (no 11) (US 2/3) needles
1 pair 3 ¼mm (no 10) (US 3) needles
1 pair 3 ¾mm (no 9) (US 5) needles

Tension

Before steaming: 24 sts and 30 rows to
10 cm measured over stocking stitch using
3 ¾mm (US 5) needles, 24 sts and 36 rows
to 10 cm measured over double moss st using
3 ¾mm (US 5) needles.

Tension note:

The Bamboo Soft yarn relaxes after steaming.
This opens the knitting and changes the
tension by approx. one stitch in the width but
does not affect the rows (23 sts and 30 rows).
Therefore your knitting, before steaming,
should have a tension of 24 sts and 30 rows
to 10 cm (over st st). Allowances are made
within the pattern for this change (see size
diagram for after relaxing measurements).

BACK

Cast on 93 (99: 105: 111: 117: 125) sts using
3 ¾mm (US 5) needles.
Row 1 (RS): K1 (0: 1: 0: 1: 1), *P1, K1; rep from *
to last 0 (1: 0: 1: 0: 0) st, P0 (1: 0: 1: 0: 0).
Row 2: As row 1.
Rows 3 and 4: P1 (0: 1: 0: 1: 1), *K1, P1; rep
from * to last 0 (1: 0: 1: 0: 0) st, K0 (1: 0: 1: 0: 0).
These 4 rows form double moss st.
Cont in double moss st, dec 1 st at each end
of 3rd and 4 (4: 4: 5: 5: 5) foll 8th rows, then
on 1 (1: 1: 0: 0: 0) foll 6th row.
81 (87: 93: 99: 105: 113) sts.
Work 0 (0: 2: 0: 2: 2) rows, ending with a **RS** row.
Next row (dec) (WS): P11 (12: 13: 14: 15:
16), *P2tog, P3, P2tog*, P to last 18 (19:
20: 21: 22: 23) sts, rep from * to * once
more, P to end.
77 (83: 89: 95: 101: 109) sts.
Change to 3mm (US 2/3) needles.
Work in garter st (knit every row) for 14 (14: 14:
18: 18: 18) rows, ending with a WS row.
Change to 3 ¾mm (US 5) needles.
Beg with a K row, work in st st for 2 rows.
Next row (inc) (RS): K3, M1, K to last 3 sts,
M1, K3.
Working all side seam increases as set by last
row, cont in st st, shaping sides by inc 1 st at
each end of 6th and 3 (3: 3: 0: 0: 0) foll 6th
rows, then on 3 (3: 3: 6: 6: 6) foll 8th rows.
93 (99: 105: 111: 117: 125) sts.
Work 9 (9: 13: 7: 9: 11) rows, ending with
a WS row.

Shape armholes

Cast off 4 sts at beg of next 2 rows.
85 (91: 97: 103: 109: 117) sts.
Dec 1 st at each end of next 5 rows, then
on foll 3 (4: 5: 5: 6: 7) alt rows, then on
foll 4th row.
67 (71: 75: 81: 85: 91) sts.
Work 14 (12: 10: 10: 8: 6) rows, ending
with a **RS** row.
Now work in double moss st, placing sts
as folls:
Row 1 (WS): K1 (1: 1: 0: 0: 1), *P1, K1; rep from *
to last 0 (0: 0: 1: 1: 0) st, P0 (0: 0: 1: 1: 0).

Row 2: As row 1.
Rows 3 and 4: P1 (1: 1: 0: 0: 1), *K1, P1; rep
from * to last 0 (0: 0: 1: 1: 0) st, K0 (0: 0: 1:
1: 0).
Last 4 rows set position of double moss st.
Cont in double moss st until armhole
measures 19 (19: 19: 21: 21: 21) cm, ending
with a WS row.

Shape shoulders and back neck

Cast off 6 (7: 7: 8: 8: 9) sts at beg of next 2 rows.
55 (57: 61: 65: 69: 73) sts.
Next row (RS): Cast off 6 (6: 7: 7: 8: 8) sts,
patt until there are 10 (10: 10: 11: 11: 12) sts
on right needle and turn, leaving rem sts on
a holder.
Work each side of neck separately.
Cast off 4 sts at beg of next row.
Cast off rem 6 (6: 6: 7: 7: 8) sts.
With RS facing rejoin yarn to rem sts, cast
off centre 23 (25: 27: 29: 31: 33) sts, patt to
end. Complete to match first side, reversing
shapings.

LEFT FRONT

Cast on 55 (58: 61: 64: 67: 71) sts using
3 ¾mm (US 5) needles.
Row 1 (RS): K1 (0: 1: 0: 1: 1), *P1, K1; rep
from * to end.
Row 2: (K1, P1) 4 times, K3, *P1, K1; rep from *
to last 0 (1: 0: 1: 0: 0) st, P0 (1: 0: 1: 0: 0).
Row 3: P1 (0: 1: 0: 1: 1), *K1, P1; rep from *
to last 10 sts, P2, (K1, P1) 4 times.
Row 4: *P1, K1; rep from * to last 1 (0: 1: 0:
1: 1) st, P1 (0: 1: 0: 1: 1).
These 4 rows set the sts.
Cont as set, dec 1 st at beg of 3rd and 4 (4: 4:
5: 5: 5) foll 8th rows, then on 1 (1: 1: 0: 0: 0)
foll 6th row.
49 (52: 55: 58: 61: 65) sts.
Work 0 (0: 2: 0: 2: 2) rows, ending with a **RS** row.
Next row (dec) (WS): P to last 18 (19: 20: 21:
22: 23) sts, P2tog, P3, P2tog, P to end.
47 (50: 53: 56: 59: 63) sts.
Change to 3mm (US 2/3) needles.
Work in garter st (knit every row) for 14 (14: 14:
18: 18: 18) rows, ending with a WS row.

Change to 3 ¾mm (US 5) needles.
Next row (RS): Knit.
Next row: (P1, K1) 5 times, P to end.
Next row (inc): K3, M1 (for side seam inc), K to last 10 sts, P2, (K1, P1) 4 times.
48 (51: 54: 57: 60: 64) sts.
Next row: (K1, P1) 4 times, K2, P to end.
Next row: K to last 10 sts, (P1, K1) 5 times.
Last 4 rows set the sts and side seam increases.
Keeping sts correct and working all side seam increases as set, cont as set, shaping side seam by inc 1 st at beg of 6th and 2 foll 6th (6th: 6th: 8th: 8th: 8th) rows.
51 (54: 57: 60: 63: 67) sts.
Work 5 (5: 5: 1: 1: 1) rows, ending with a WS row.
Shape front slope
Next row (RS): (K3, M1 · for side seam inc) 1 (1: 1: 0: 0: 0) times, K to last 12 sts, K2tog tbl (for front slope dec), patt 10 sts.
51 (54: 57: 59: 62: 66) sts.
Working all front slope decreases as set by last row, dec 1 st at front slope edge of 4th and 0 (3: 6: 6: 8: 9) foll 4th rows, then on 4 (2: 1: 1: 0: 0) foll 6th rows **and at same time** inc 1 st at side seam edge of 8th (8th: 8th: 6th: 6th: 6th) and 2 (2: 2: 3: 3: 3) foll 8th rows.
49 (51: 52: 55: 57: 60) sts.
Work 5 (5: 3: 3: 3: 1) rows, ending with a WS row.
Shape armhole
Cast off 4 sts at beg and dec 1 (1: 0: 0: 1: 0) st at front slope edge of next row.
44 (46: 48: 51: 52: 56) sts.
Work 1 row.
Dec 1 st at armhole edge of next 5 rows, then on foll 3 (4: 5: 5: 6: 7) alt rows, then on foll 4th row a**nd at same time** dec 1 st at front slope edge of 5th (5th: next: next: 5th: next) and 0 (0: 0: 0: 0: 2) foll 4th rows, then on 1 (2: 3: 3: 2: 2) foll 6th rows.
33 (33: 33: 36: 37: 38) sts.
Dec 1 st at front slope edge **only** on 2nd (6th: 6th: 6th: 2nd: 4th) and 2 (1: 0: 0: 1: 0) foll 6th rows. 30 (31: 32: 35: 35: 37) sts.
Work 0 (0: 4: 4: 0: 2) rows, ending with a **RS** row.
Now work as folls:
Row 1 (WS): Patt 10 sts, K0 (1: 0: 0: 0: 1), *P1, K1; rep from * to last 0 (0: 0: 1: 1: 0) st, P0 (0: 0: 1: 1: 0).
Row 2: P0 (0: 0: 1: 1: 0), *K1, P1; rep from * to last 10 (11: 10: 10: 10: 11) sts, K0 (1: 0: 0: 0: 1), patt 10 sts.

Row 3: Patt 10 sts, P0 (1: 0: 0: 0: 1), *K1, P1; rep from * to last 0 (0: 0: 1: 1: 0) st, K0 (0: 0: 1: 1: 0).
Row 4: K0 (0: 0: 1: 1: 0), *P1, K1; rep from * to last 10 (11: 10: 10: 10: 11) sts, P0 (1: 0: 0: 0: 1), patt 10 sts.
Last 4 rows set the sts.
Cont as set, dec 1 st at front slope edge of 6th (6th: 2nd: 2nd: 6th: 4th) and 1 (1: 1: 2: 1: 1) foll 10th rows.
28 (29: 30: 32: 33: 35) sts.
Cont straight until left front matches back to beg of shoulder shaping, ending with a WS row.
Shape shoulder
Cast off 6 (7: 7: 8: 8: 9) sts at beg of next row, 6 (6: 7: 7: 8: 8) sts at beg of foll alt row, then 6 (6: 6: 7: 7: 8) sts at beg of foll alt row.
10 sts.
Cont in patt on these 10 sts only (for back neck border extension) for a further 6.5 (7: 7.5: 8: 8.5: 9) cm, ending with a WS row.
Cast off.
Mark positions for 3 buttons along left front opening edge – first to come in row 7 (7: 7: 9: 9: 9) of waist garter st section, last to come level with start of front slope shaping, and rem button to come midway between first 2 buttons.

RIGHT FRONT
Cast on 55 (58: 61: 64: 67: 71) sts using 3 ¾mm (US 5) needles.
Row 1 (RS): *K1, P1; rep from * to last 1 (0: 1: 0: 1: 1) st, K1 (0: 1: 0: 1: 1).
Row 2: P0 (1: 0: 1: 0: 0), *K1, P1; rep from * to last 11 sts, K3, (P1, K1) 4 times.
Row 3: (P1, K1) 4 times, P2, *P1, K1; rep from * to last 1 (0: 1: 0: 1: 1) st, P1 (0: 1: 0: 1: 1).
Row 4: P1 (0: 1: 0: 1: 1), *K1, P1; rep from * to end.
These 4 rows set the sts.
Cont as set, dec 1 st at end of 3rd and 4 (4: 4: 5: 5: 5) foll 8th rows, then on 1 (1: 1: 0: 0: 0) foll 6th row.
49 (52: 55: 58: 61: 65) sts.
Work 0 (0: 2: 0: 2: 2) rows, ending with a **RS** row.
Next row (dec) (WS): P11 (12: 13: 14: 15: 16), P2tog, P3, P2tog, P to end.
47 (50: 53: 56: 59: 63) sts.
Change to 3mm (US 2/3) needles.
Work in garter st (knit every row) for 6 (6: 6: 8: 8: 8) rows, ending with a WS row.

Next row (buttonhole row) (RS): Patt 3 sts, cast off 3 sts (to make a buttonhole – cast on 3 sts over these cast-off sts on next row), patt to end.
Working a further 2 buttonholes in this way to correspond with positions marked for buttons on left front and noting that no further reference will be made to buttonholes, cont as folls:
Work in garter st (knit every row) for 7 (7: 7: 9: 9: 9) rows more, ending with a WS row.
Change to 3 ¾mm (US 5) needles.
Next row (RS): Knit.
Next row: P to end 10 sts, (K1, P1) 5 times.
Next row (inc): (P1, K1) 4 times, P2, K to last 3 sts, M1 (for side seam inc), K3.
48 (51: 54: 57: 60: 64) sts.
Next row: P to last 10 sts, K2, (P1, K1) 4 times.
Next row: (K1, P1) 5 times, K to end.
Last 4 rows set the sts and side seam increases.
Keeping sts correct and working all side seam increases as set, cont as set, shaping side seam by inc 1 st at end of 6th and 2 foll 6th (6th: 6th: 8th: 8th: 8th) rows.
51 (54: 57: 60: 63: 67) sts.
Work 5 (5: 5: 1: 1: 1) rows, ending with a WS row.
Shape front slope
Next row (RS): Patt 10 sts, K2tog (for front slope dec), K to last 3 (3: 3: 0: 0: 0) sts, (M1 · for side seam inc, K3) 1 (1: 1: 0: 0: 0) times.
51 (54: 57: 59: 62: 66) sts.
Working all front slope decreases as set by last row, complete to match left front, reversing shapings.

3/4 length sleeves (both alike)
Cast on 55 (57: 59: 63: 65: 67) sts using 3 ¼mm (US 3) needles.
Work in garter st (knit every row) for 10 (10: 10: 12: 12: 12) rows, ending with a WS row.
Change to 3 ¾mm (US 5) needles.
Next row (inc) (RS): K3, M1, K to last 3 sts, M1, K3.
Working all increases as set by last row and beg with a P row, cont in st st, shaping sides by inc 1 st at each end of 10th (10th: 10th: 12th: 12th: 12th) and 1 (1: 1: 0: 0: 0) foll 10th row, then on 5 (5: 5: 6: 6: 6) foll 12th rows.
71 (73: 75: 79: 81: 83) sts.
Cont straight until sleeve measures 32 (33: 34: 35: 36: 37) cm, ending with a WS row.

Shape top

Cast off 4 sts at beg of next 2 rows.
63 (65: 67: 71: 73: 75) sts.
Dec 1 st at each end of next 3 rows, then
on foll alt row, then on 5 (5: 5: 6: 6: 6) foll
4th rows, then on foll 5 (5: 5: 6: 6: 5) alt
rows, then on foll 3 (3: 3: 3: 3: 5) rows,
ending with a WS row.
29 (31: 33: 33: 35: 35) sts.
Cast off 4 sts at beg of next 2 rows.
Cast off rem 21 (23: 25: 25: 27: 27) sts.

Angel wing sleeves (both alike)

Cast on 191 (191: 191: 207: 207: 207) sts
using 3mm (US 2/3) needles.
Row 1 (RS): K1, *P1, K1; rep from * to end.
Row 2: As row 1.
Rows 3 and 4: P1, *K1, P1; rep from * to end.
These 4 rows form double moss st.
Work in double moss st for a further 2 rows,
ending with a WS row.
Change to 3 ¾mm (US 5) needles.
Beg with a K row, work in st st for 6 rows,
ending with a WS row.

Shape top

Place marker on centre st of last row.
Counting out both ways from marker, *leave
22 (22: 22: 24: 24: 24) sts then place marker
on next st; rep from * twice more. 7 markers
in total, and 26 (26: 26: 28: 28: 28) sts
beyond edge markers.
Next row (RS): Cast off 2 sts, *K to within
1 st of marked st, slip 2 sts as though to
K2tog, K1, pass 2 slipped sts over; rep from *
6 times more, K to end.
Cast off 2 sts at beg of next row.
173 (173: 173: 189: 189: 189) sts.
Dec 1 st at each end of next 3 rows.
167 (167: 167: 183: 183: 183) sts.
Work 1 row.
Next row (dec) (RS): K2tog, *K to within
1 st of marked st, slip 2 sts as though to
K2tog, K1, pass 2 slipped sts over; rep from *
6 times more, K to last 2 sts, K2tog.
Work 5 rows.
Rep last 6 rows 8 (8: 8: 9: 9: 9) times more.
23 sts.
Work 5 rows, ending with a WS row.
Next row (RS): K1, (slip 2 sts as though
to K2tog, K1, pass 2 slipped sts over)
7 times, K1.
Next row: P2tog, P to last 2 sts, P2tog.
Cast off rem 7 sts.

MAKING UP

Pin out the pieces and **steam** gently without
allowing the iron to touch the yarn.
Join both shoulder seams using back stitch,
or mattress stitch if preferred. Join cast-off
ends of back neck border extensions, then
sew one row-end edge in place to back neck
edge. Join side seams.
Join sleeve seams. Set in sleeves. Sew on
buttons.

Button frames

Thread a needle with two strands of yarn.
Secure yarn to centre back of button, and
then using the diagram as a guide, weave the
yarn around the framework of the button.
Fasten off securely.

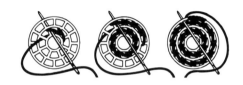

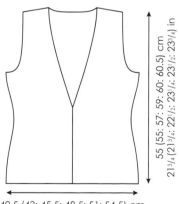

40.5 (43: 45.5: 48.5: 51: 54.5) cm
16 (17: 18: 19: 20: 21½) in

55 (55: 57: 59: 60: 60.5) cm
21¾ (21¾: 22½: 23¼: 23½: 23¾) in

32 (33: 34: 35: 36: 37) cm
12½ (13: 13½: 13¾: 14¼: 14½) in

PRUDENCE
UNDERSTATED SWEATER WITH WIDE NECK & FULL SLEEVES

Recommendation
Suitable for the knitter with a little experience.
Please see page 16 for photograph.

	XS	S	M	L	XL	XXL	
To fit	**81**	**86**	**91**	**97**	**102**	**109**	cm
bust	32	34	36	38	40	43	in

Rowan Classic Bamboo Soft
11 12 13 14 15 16 x 50gm
Photographed in Mystic ᴷ
ᴷ Kim Hargreaves for Rowan Classic

Needles
1 pair 3mm (no 11) (US 2/3) needles
1 pair 3 ¼mm (no 10) (US 3) needles
1 pair 3 ¾mm (no 9) (US 5) needles
3mm (no 11) (US 2/3) circular needle
3 ¼mm (no 10) (US 3) circular needle

Tension
Before steaming: 24 sts and 30 rows to
10 cm measured over stocking stitch using
3 ¾mm (US 5) needles.

Tension note:
The Bamboo Soft yarn relaxes after steaming.
This opens the knitting and changes the
tension by approximately one stitch in the
width but does not affect the rows (23 sts
and 30 rows). Therefore your knitting,
before steaming, should have a tension of
24 sts and 30 rows to 10 cm. Allowances
have been made within the pattern for this
change (see size diagram for after relaxing
measurements).

BACK AND FRONT (both the same)
Cast on 97 (103: 109: 115: 121: 129) sts
using 3 ¼mm (US 3) needles.
Work in garter st for 10 rows, ending with
a WS row.
Change to 3 ¾mm (US 5) needles.
Beg with a K row, work in st st for 4 rows.
Beg with a P row, work in rev st st for
2 rows.
Beg with a K row, work in st st for 6 rows.
Beg with a P row, work in rev st st for 2 rows,
dec 1 (1: 1: 0: 0: 0) st at each end of first of
these rows.
95 (101: 107: 115: 121: 129) sts.
Beg with a K row, work in st st for 4 (4: 4: 6:
6: 6) rows, dec 0 (0: 0: 1: 1: 1) st at each end
of first of these rows.
95 (101: 107: 113: 119: 127) sts.
Next row (dec) (RS): K2, K2tog, K to last
4 sts, K2tog tbl, K2.
Working all further side seam decreases as
set by last row, cont as follows:
Work in st st for 3 (3: 3: 1: 1: 1) rows more.
Beg with a P row, work in rev st st for 2 rows.
Beg with a K row, cont in st st throughout as
follows:
Dec 1 st at each end of next (next: next: 3rd:
3rd: 3rd) and 4 foll 8th rows.
83 (89: 95: 101: 107: 115) sts.
Work 17 rows, ending with a WS row.
Next row (inc) (RS): K2, M1, K to last 2 sts,
M1, K2.
Working all side seam increases as set by last
row, inc 1 st at each end of 6th and 3 foll 6th
rows, then on 3 foll 8th rows.
99 (105: 111: 117: 123: 131) sts.
Cont straight until back measures 43 (43: 44:
45: 46: 46) cm, ending with a WS row.
Shape raglan armholes
Cast off 4 (5: 5: 5: 6: 6) sts at beg of next
2 rows.
91 (95: 101: 107: 111: 119) sts.
Work 2 (2: 0: 0: 0: 0) rows.
L, XL and XXL sizes
Next row (RS): K1, K2tog, K to last 3 sts,
K2tog tbl, K1.

Next row: P1, P2tog tbl, P to last 3 sts,
P2tog, P1.
Rep last 2 rows – (·: ·: 0: 1: 2) times more.
· (·: ·: 103: 103: 107) sts.
All sizes
Next row (RS): K1, K2tog, K to last 3 sts,
K2tog tbl, K1.
Working all raglan armhole decreases as set
by last row, dec 1 st at each end of 2nd (4th:
2nd: 2nd: 2nd: 2nd) and foll 8 (9: 11: 11: 10:
11) alt rows.
71 (73: 75: 77: 79: 81) sts.
Work 1 row, ending with a WS row.
Cast off.

SLEEVES (both alike)
Cast on 97 (99: 103: 105: 107: 109) sts using
3 ¾mm (US 5) needles.
Beg with a K row, work in st st for 4 rows.
Beg with a P row, work in rev st st for 2 rows.
Beg with a K row, work in st st for 6 rows, dec
1 st at each end of first of these rows.
95 (97: 101: 103: 105: 107) sts.
Beg with a P row, work in rev st st for 2 rows,
dec 1 st at each end of first of these rows.
93 (95: 99: 101: 103: 105) sts.
Beg with a K row, work in st st for 8 rows, dec
1 st at each end of 5th of these rows.
91 (93: 97: 99: 101: 103) sts.
Beg with a P row, work in rev st st for 2 rows.
Beg with a K row, work in st st for 10 rows,
dec 1 st at each end of first and 7th of
these rows.
87 (89: 93: 95: 97: 99) sts.
Beg with a P row, work in rev st st for
2 rows.
Beg with a K row, cont in st st throughout
as follows:
Dec 1 st at each end of next and 4 foll
6th rows, then on foll 8th row, then on foll
12th (12th: 12th: 14th: 14th: 14th) row,
then on foll 14th (14th: 14th: 18th: 18th:
18th) row.
71 (73: 77: 79: 81: 83) sts.
Cont straight until sleeve measures 40 (41:
42: 43: 44: 45) cm, ending with a WS row.

Shape raglan

Cast off 4 (5: 5: 5: 6: 6) sts at beg of next 2 rows.

63 (63: 67: 69: 69: 71) sts.

Working all raglan decreases as set by back and front, dec 1 st at each end of 3rd and 1 (3: 2: 2: 4: 6) foll 4th rows, then on foll 8 (5: 7: 7: 4: 2) alt rows.

43 (45: 47: 49: 51: 53) sts.

Work 1 row, ending with a WS row.

Cast off.

Cuffs (both alike)

With RS facing and using 3mm (US 2/3) needles, pick up and knit 97 (99: 103: 105: 107: 109) sts from cast-on edge of sleeve.

Row 1 (WS): P2 (1: 3: 2: 5: 4), (P2tog) 47 (49: 49: 51: 49: 51) times, P1 (0: 2: 1: 4: 3).

50 (50: 54: 54: 58: 58) sts.

Row 2: K2, *P2, K2; rep from * to end.

Row 3: P2, *K2, P2; rep from * to end.

Rep last 2 rows until cuff measures 7 cm from pick-up row.

Cast off in rib.

MAKING UP

Pin out the pieces and **steam** gently without allowing the iron to touch the yarn.

Join both front and right back raglan seams using back stitch, or mattress stitch if preferred.

Neckband

With RS facing and using 3 ¼mm (US 3) circular needle, pick up and knit 40 (42: 44: 46: 48: 50) sts across top of left sleeve placing a marker between centre 2 sts of these sts, place another marker on needle, pick up and knit 70 (72: 74: 76: 78: 80) sts across front neck, place another marker on needle, pick up and knit 40 (42: 44: 46: 48: 50) sts across top of right sleeve placing a marker between centre 2 sts of these sts, place another marker on needle, then pick up and knit 70 (72: 74: 76: 78: 80) sts across back neck.

220 (228: 236: 244: 252: 260) sts.

(5 markers in total.)

Row 1 (WS): (Knit to marker, slip marker to right needle) to end.

Cont in garter st, taking markers up the knitting, and shape neck as follows:

Work 4 rows.

Row 6 (dec) (RS): K2, K2tog tbl, *K to 3 sts before next marker, K2tog, K2 (marker is between these 2 sts), K2tog tbl; rep from * 4 times more, K to last 4 sts, K2tog, K2.

208 (216: 224: 232: 240: 248) sts.

Work 3 rows.

Row 10: As row 6.

Work 1 row.

Rep last 2 rows once more, then row 6 again.

172 (180: 188: 196: 204: 212) sts.

Change to 3mm (US 2/3) circular needle.

Work 1 row, ending with a WS row.

Row 16: As row 6.

Work 1 row.

Row 18: As row 6.

148 (156: 164: 172: 180: 188) sts.

Work 2 rows.

Cast off knitwise (on **WS**), casting off quite firmly across sts at top of sleeves.

Join left back raglan and neckband seam. Join side and sleeve seams.

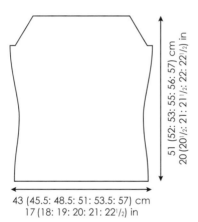

43 (45.5: 48.5: 51: 53.5: 57) cm
17 (18: 19: 20: 21: 22½) in

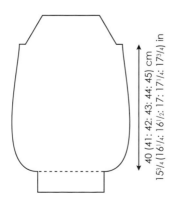

Please note:

These measurements do not include the neck edging.

SPLENDOUR
CROPPED CARDIGAN WITH SINGLE BUTTON

Recommendation
Suitable for the knitter with a little experience.
Please see pages 17, 48 & 49 for photographs.

	XS	S	M	L	XL	XXL	
To fit	**81**	**86**	**91**	**97**	**101**	**107**	**cm**
bust	32	34	36	38	40	42	in

Rowan Kid Classic
7 7 7 7 8 9 x 50gm
Photographed in Dashing^K

^K Kim Hargreaves for Rowan

Buttons – 1

Needles
1 pair 3¾ mm (no 9) (US 5) needles
1 pair 4½ mm (no 7) (US 7) needles

Tension
21 sts and 27 rows to 10 cm measured over
stocking stitch using 4½ mm (US 7) needles.

Special abbreviation
MP = Make picot: cast on 1 st, cast off 1 st.
(See information page for details)

MAIN KNITTING
(knitted from right cuff to left cuff)
Right sleeve
Cast on 54 (56: 58: 60: 62: 64) sts using
4½ mm (US 7) needles and, beg with a K row,
cont in st st as folls:
Work 2 rows.
Inc 8 sts evenly across next row.
62 (64: 66: 68: 70: 72) sts.
Work 11 rows, ending with a WS row.
Next row (RS) (inc): K2, M1, K to last 2 sts,
M1, K2. 64 (66: 68: 70: 72: 74) sts.
Work 13 rows.
Inc 1 st as before at each end of next row,
then on 3 (3: 3: 4: 4: 4) foll 14th rows, then
on foll 12th row. 74 (76: 78: 82: 84: 86) sts.
Work 9 rows.
Inc 1 st as before at each end of next row and
foll 10th (10th: 10th: 4th: 6th: 8th) row.
78 (80: 82: 86: 88: 90) sts.
Work 1 row, ending with a WS row.
Shape side
Inc 1 st at each end of next row and 3 (3: 4:
1: 2: 2) foll alt rows.
86 (88: 92: 90: 94: 96) sts.
Work 1 row, ending with a WS row.
Cast on 3 (4: 5: 2: 2: 3) sts at beg of next
2 rows and 6 sts at beg of next 8 (8: 8: 10:
10: 10) rows, ending with a WS row.
140 (144: 150: 154: 158: 162) sts.
Work right front and back
Work 19 (21: 25: 27: 27: 29) rows, ending
with a **RS** row.
Shape lower right front
Dec 1 st at end of next row and 3 (2: 3: 3:
4: 4) foll alt rows.
136 (141: 146: 150: 153: 157) sts.
Divide for neck
Next row (RS) (dec): K until there are 56 (60:
60: 62: 65: 67) sts on right needle and turn,
leaving rem sts on a holder for back.
Work back and front separately.
Next row (WS): Cast off 5 (5: 5: 6: 4: 4) sts
at beg and dec 1 st at end of row.
50 (54: 54: 56: 60: 62) sts.
Work 1 row.

Cast off 3 sts at beg and dec 1 st at end of
next row and 2(3: 3: 2: 2: 2) foll alt rows.
38 (38: 38: 43: 48: 50) sts.
Next row (RS)(dec): Dec 1 st work to end.
Next row: Cast off 3 sts at beg and dec 1 st
at end of row.
33 (33: 33: 38: 43: 45) sts.
Rep the last 2 rows 1 (1: 1: 2: 3: 3) times
more.
28 (28: 28: 28: 28: 30) sts.
Cast off 3 sts at beg of next 4 rows.
16 (16: 16: 16: 16: 18) sts.
Cast off.
With RS facing rejoin yarn to rem 80 (81: 86:
88: 88: 90) sts, cast off centre 11 (10: 12:
12: 10: 10) sts, K to end.
69 (71: 74: 76: 78: 80) sts.
Dec 1 st at neck edge on next 4 rows, ending
with a **RS** row.
65 (67: 70: 72: 74: 76) sts.
Work 35 (37: 37: 39: 39: 43) rows, ending
with a WS row.
Inc 1 st at neck edge on next 4 rows, ending
with a WS row.
69 (71: 74: 76: 78: 80) sts.
Leave sts on a spare needle.
Left front
Cast on 16 (16: 16: 16: 16: 18) sts using
4½ mm (US 7) needles and, beg with a K row,
cont in st st as folls:
Work 1 row.
Cast on 3 sts at beg of next 4 rows.
28 (28: 28: 28: 28: 30) sts.
Next row (WS): Cast on 3 sts at beg and inc
1 st at end of row.
Next row: Inc 1 st, K to end.
33 (33: 33: 33: 33: 35) sts.
Rep last 2 rows 1 (1: 1: 2: 3: 3) times more.
38 (38: 38: 43: 48: 50) sts.
Cast on 3 sts at beg and inc 1 st at end of
next row and 2 (3: 3: 2: 2: 2) foll alt rows.
50 (54: 54: 55: 60: 62) sts
Work 1 row.
Next row (WS): Cast on 5 (5: 5: 6: 4: 4) sts at
beg and inc 1 st at end of row.
56 (60: 60: 62: 65: 67) sts.

Join front and back together

Next row (RS): K56 (60: 60: 62: 65: 67) sts, cast on 11 (10: 12: 12: 10: 10) sts, K across 69 (71: 74: 76: 78: 80) sts on spare needle. 136 (141: 146: 150: 153: 157) sts.

Inc 1 st at end of next row and foll 3 (2: 3: 3: 4: 4) alt rows.

140 (144: 150: 154: 158: 162) sts.

Work 20 (22: 26: 28: 28: 30) rows, ending with a WS row.

Shape sides

Cast off 6 sts at beg of next 8 (8: 8: 10: 10: 10) rows, and then 3 (4: 5: 2: 2: 3) sts at beg of next 2 rows.

86 (88: 92: 90: 94: 96)sts.

Next row (RS) (dec): K2, K2tog, K to last 4 sts, K2tog tbl, K2.

84 (86: 90: 88: 92: 94) sts.

Work 1 row.

Dec 1 st at each end of next row and 3 (3: 4: 1: 2: 2) foll alt rows.

76 (78: 80: 84: 86: 88) sts.

Left sleeve

Work 9 (9: 9: 3: 5: 5) rows.

Dec 1 st at each end of next row and foll 10th row, then on foll 12th row, then on 4 (4: 4: 5: 5:5) foll 14th rows.

62 (64: 66: 68: 70: 72) sts.

Work 10 rows, ending with a RS row.

Dec 8 sts evenly across next row.

54 (56: 56: 60: 62: 64) sts.

Work 2 rows.

Cast off.

MAKING UP

Press using a warm iron over a damp cloth.

Join underarm and side seam, preferably using mattress st.

Place a marker for the buttonhole on the right front, half way across the 16 (16: 16: 16: 16: 18) sts cast-off at centre front edge.

Front edging

Cast on 14 (15: 15: 16: 16: 17) sts, using 3¾ mm (US 9) needles.

Row 1 (RS): MP, knit to end.

Row 2: Purl.

Row 3: MP, purl to end.

Row 4: Knit.

These 4 rows form patt and are rep throughout.

Cont in pattern until edging fits neatly and not **stretched** from right side seam to buttonhole marker on right front, ending with row 4.

Slip stitch neatly into place.

Buttonhole row (RS): MP, K until 7 sts on right needle, cast off 3 sts, K to end.

Next row: Work across row in patt, casting-on 3 sts over those cast-off on previous row.

14 (15: 15: 16: 16: 17) sts.

Cont in patt until band fits up right front to shoulder, across back neck, down and around left front to left side seam and across lower back to right side seam.

Slip stitch neatly into place, stretching edging slightly across lower back, and adjusting length if necessary.

Cast off.

Join ends of edging neatly together.

Cuffs (make 2)

Cast on 22 (23: 23: 24: 24: 25) sts using 3¾ mm (US 9) needles.

Row 1 (RS): MP, knit to end.

Row 2: Purl.

Row 3: MP, purl to end.

Shape side

Short row shaping (WS): Knit 7 sts, wrap next stitch (by slipping next st onto right needle, bring yarn to front of work between needles and the slip same st back onto left needle), turn and K to end.

Short row shaping: Purl 14 sts, wrap next stitch, turn and P to end.

Row 4: Knit.

Cont in pattern as for front edging for a further 47 (47: 47: 51: 51: 51) rows, ending with patt row 3.

Shape side

Short row shaping (WS): Knit 14 sts, wrap next stitch, turn and K to end.

Short row shaping: Purl 7 sts, wrap next stitch, turn and P to end.

Work 2 rows. Cast off.

Join seam.

Stitch the straight edge of the cuff neatly into place around lower edge of sleeve, easing the sleeve into the cuff. Sew on button.

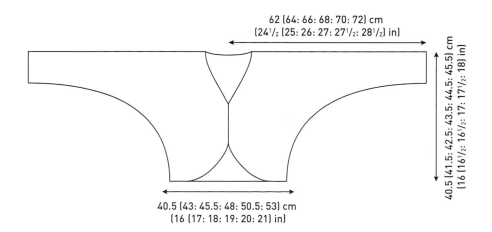

62 (64: 66: 68: 70: 72) cm
(24½ (25: 26: 27: 27½: 28½) in)

40.5 (41.5: 42.5: 43.5: 44.5: 45.5) cm
(16 (16½: 16½: 17: 17½: 18) in)

40.5 (43: 45.5: 48: 50.5: 53) cm
(16 (17: 18: 19: 20: 21) in)

PAISLEY

FITTED CABLED JACKET WITH SHAPED PEPLUM

Recommendation

Suitable for the more experience knitter.
Please see pages 20 & 22 for photographs.

	XS	S	M	L	XL	XXL	
To fit	**81**	**86**	**91**	**97**	**102**	**109**	cm
bust	32	34	36	38	40	43	in

Rowan Classic Cashsoft Chunky

18 19 20 21 22 24 x 50gm
Photographed in Eggplant

Buttons – 5

Needles

1 pair 6 ½mm (no 3) (US 10 ½) needles
1 pair 7mm (no 2) (US 10 ½/11) needles
Cable needle

Tension

14 sts and 20 rows to 10 cm measured over
textured pattern using 7mm (US 10 ½/11)
needles

Special abbreviations

cn = cable needle; **Cr4R** = slip next st onto cn
and leave at back of work, K3, then P1 from
cn; **Cr4L** = slip next 3 sts onto cn and leave
at front of work, P1, then K3 from cn; **C6B** =
slip next 3 sts onto cn and leave at back of
work, K3, then K3 from cn; **C6F** = slip next
3 sts onto cn and leave at front of work, K3,
then K3 from cn.

Pattern note: When casting off across top of
cables, work K2tog 3 times (or twice, depending
on position in patt) to reduce the number of sts
in seam. The number of sts stated in patt relates
to the actual number of sts cast off.

BACK

Cast on 71 (73: 77: 81: 85: 89) sts using
7mm (US 10 ½/11) needles.
Row 1 (RS): P0 (0: 0: 1: 0: 0), (K1 tbl, P1) 5
(5: 6: 6: 7: 8) times, inc once in each of next 3
sts, P1, (K1 tbl, P1) 4 times, inc once in each
of next 3 sts, P1, (K1 tbl, P1) 10 (11: 11:
12: 13: 13) times, inc once in each of next
3 sts, wrap next st (by slipping next st on
left needle onto right needle, taking yarn to
opposite side of work between needles and
then slipping same st back onto left needle
– when working back across wrapped sts,
work the wrapped st and the wrapping loop
tog as 1 st) and turn.
Row 2: P6, K21 (23: 23: 25: 27: 27), P6, K9,
P6, wrap next st and turn.
Row 3: K6, P1, (K1 tbl, P1) 4 times, K6, P1,
(K1 tbl, P1) 10 (11: 11: 12: 13: 13) times, K6,
P1, (K1 tbl, P1) 4 times, inc once in each of
next 3 sts, wrap next st and turn.
Row 4: P6, K9, P6, K21 (23: 23: 25: 27: 27),
P6, K9, P6, wrap next st and turn.
Row 5: K6, P1, (K1 tbl, P1) 4 times, K6, P1,
(K1 tbl, P1) 10 (11: 11: 12: 13: 13) times, K6,
P1, (K1 tbl, P1) 4 times, K6, (P1, K1 tbl) 5 (5:
6: 6: 7: 8) times, P0 (0: 0: 1: 0: 0).
Row 6: K10 (10: 12: 13: 14: 16), P6, K9, P6,
K21 (23: 23: 25: 27: 27), P6, K9, P6, K10
(10: 12: 13: 14: 16).
83 (85: 89: 93: 97: 101) sts.
Now work in patt as folls:
Row 1 (RS): P0 (0: 0: 1: 0: 0), (K1 tbl, P1)
5 (5: 6: 6: 7: 8) times, K6, place marker on
needle, P1, (K1 tbl, P1) 4 times, place marker
on needle, K6, P1, (K1 tbl, P1) 10 (11: 11:
12: 13: 13) times, K6, place marker on
needle, P1, (K1 tbl, P1) 4 times, place marker
on needle, K6, (P1, K1 tbl) 5 (5: 6: 6: 7: 8)
times, P0 (0: 0: 1: 0: 0). (4 markers in total.)

Taking markers up work, cont as folls:
Row 2: K10 (10: 12: 13: 14: 16), P6, K9, P6,
K21 (23: 23: 25: 27: 27), P6, K9, P6, K10
(10: 12: 13: 14: 16).
These 2 rows set the sts – 4 panels of 6 sts in st
st (for cables) and all other sts in textured patt.
Keeping sts correct as set, work 2 (2: 2: 4:
6: 6) rows.
Next row (RS): Patt to within 6 sts of first
marker, C6B, patt to next marker, C6B, patt
to within 6 sts of next marker, C6F, patt to
next marker, C6F, patt to end.
Work 1 row.
Next row (dec) (RS): *Patt to marker, P2tog,
patt to within 2 sts of next marker, P2tog tbl;
rep from * once more, patt to end.
79 (81: 85: 89: 93: 97) sts.
(**Note:** After decs have been worked between
markers, work the resulting st as a P st on RS
rows and as a K st on WS rows.)
Work 5 rows.
Next row (RS): Patt to within 6 sts of first
marker, C6B, patt to next marker, C6B, patt
to within 6 sts of next marker, C6F, patt to
next marker, C6F, patt to end.
Work 1 row.
Next row (dec) (RS): Work 2 tog, *patt to
marker, P2tog, patt to within 2 sts of next marker,
P2tog tbl; rep from * once more, patt to last
2 sts, work 2 tog.
73 (75: 79: 83: 87: 91) sts.
Work 5 rows.
Next row (dec) (RS): Patt to within 6 sts of
first marker, C6B, P2tog, patt to within 2
sts of next marker, P2tog tbl, C6B, patt to
within 6 sts of next marker, C6F, P2tog, patt
to within 2 sts of next marker, P2tog tbl, C6F,
patt to end.
69 (71: 75: 79: 83: 87) sts.
Work 3 rows.
Next row (dec) (RS): Work 2 tog, (patt to
marker, P3tog) twice, patt to last 2 sts,
work 2 tog.
63 (65: 69: 73: 77: 81) sts.
Work 3 rows.
Change to 6 ½mm (US 10 ½) needles.

Next row (RS): Patt to within 6 sts of first marker, C6B, patt to next marker (this is just 1 st at this point), C6B, patt to within 6 sts of next marker, C6F, patt to next marker (this is just 1 st at this point), C6F, patt to end.
Work 5 rows.
Next row (RS): Patt to first marker, inc in st between this marker and next marker, patt to next marker, inc in st between this marker and next marker, patt to end.
65 (67: 71: 75: 79: 83) sts.
Next row: Patt to first marker, M1, K2, M1, slip next marker to right needle, patt to 3rd marker, M1, K2, M1, patt to end.
69 (71: 75: 79: 83: 87) sts.
Remove markers.
Change to 7mm (US 10 ½/11) needles.
Now place charts as folls:
Row 1 (RS): Patt 6 (6: 8: 9: 10: 12) sts, work next 20 sts as row 1 of chart A, patt 17 (19: 19: 21: 23: 23) sts, work next 20 sts as row 1 of chart B, patt 6 (6: 8: 9: 10: 12) sts.
Row 2: Patt 6 (6: 8: 9: 10: 12) sts, work next 20 sts as row 2 of chart B, patt 17 (19: 19: 21: 23: 23) sts, work next 20 sts as row 2 of chart A, patt 6 (6: 8: 9: 10: 12) sts.
These 2 rows set the sts – cable panels with textured st between and at sides.
Cont as set, shaping side seams by inc 1 st at each end of 3rd and 3 foll 8th rows, taking inc sts into textured patt.
77 (79: 83: 87: 91: 95) sts.
Work 5 (5: 7: 7: 7: 7) rows, ending with a WS row.

Shape armholes
Keeping patt correct, cast off 3 sts at beg of next 2 rows.
71 (73: 77: 81: 85: 89) sts.
Dec 1 st at each end of next 3 (3: 5: 5: 5: 5) rows, then on foll 3 (3: 2: 3: 3: 4) alt rows.
59 (61: 63: 65: 69: 71) sts.
Cont straight until armhole measures 18 (19: 19: 20: 21: 22) cm, ending with a WS row.
Shape shoulders and back neck
Cast off 7 sts at beg of next 2 rows.
45 (47: 49: 51: 55: 57) sts.
Next row (RS): Cast off 7 (6: 7: 7: 7: 7) sts, patt until there are 10 (11: 10: 10: 11: 11) sts on right needle and turn, leaving rem sts on a holder.
Work each side of neck separately.
Cast off 4 sts at beg of next row.
Cast off rem 6 (7: 6: 6: 7: 7) sts.
With RS facing rejoin yarn to rem sts, cast off centre 11 (13: 15: 17: 19: 21) sts, patt to end. Complete to match first side, reversing shapings.

LEFT FRONT
Cast on 42 (42: 44: 46: 48: 50) sts using 7mm (US 10 ½/11) needles.
Row 1 (RS): P0 (0: 0: 1: 0: 0), (K1 tbl, P1) 5 (5: 6: 6: 7: 8) times, wrap next st and turn.
Row 2: K10 (10: 12: 13: 14: 16).
Row 3: P0 (0: 0: 1: 0: 0), (K1 tbl, P1) 5 (5: 6: 7: 8) times, inc once in each of next 3 sts, P1, (K1 tbl, P1) 4 times, wrap next st and turn.

Row 4: K9, P6, K10 (10: 12: 13: 14: 16).
Row 5: P0 (0: 0: 1: 0: 0), (K1 tbl, P1) 5 (5: 6: 6: 7: 8) times, K6, P1, (K1 tbl, P1) 4 times, inc once in each of next 3 sts, P1, (K1 tbl, P1) 5 times, P6 (6: 6: 7: 8: 8).
Row 6: K17 (17: 17: 19: 21: 21), P6, K9, P6, K10 (10: 12: 13: 14: 16).
48 (48: 50: 52: 54: 56) sts.
Now work in patt as folls:
Row 1 (RS): P0 (0: 0: 1: 0: 0), (K1 tbl, P1) 5 (5: 6: 6: 7: 8) times, (C6B) 1 (1: 1: 0: 0: 0) times, K0 (0: 0: 6: 6: 6), place marker on needle, P1, (K1 tbl, P1) 4 times, place marker on needle, (C6B) 1 (1: 1: 0: 0: 0) times, K0 (0: 0: 6: 6: 6), P1, (K1 tbl, P1) 5 times, K6 (6: 6: 7: 8: 8).
(2 markers in total.)
Taking markers up work, cont as folls:
Row 2: P6 (6: 6: 7: 8: 8), K11, P6, K9, P6, K10 (10: 12: 13: 14: 16).
These 2 rows set position of textured patt between markers and at side seam edge.
Keeping textured patt correct, cont as folls:
Row 3: Patt 10 (10: 12: 13: 14: 16) sts, (C6B) 0 (0: 0: 1: 0: 0) times, K6 (6: 6: 0: 6: 6), (P2tog, patt 5 sts, P2tog tbl) 1 (1: 1: 0: 0: 0) times, patt 0 (0: 0: 9: 9: 9) sts, (C6B) 0 (0: 0: 1: 0: 0) times, K6 (6: 6: 0: 6: 6), P1, (K1 tbl, P1) 5 times, P6 (6: 6: 7: 8: 8).
46 (46: 48: 52: 54: 56) sts.
Row 4: K17 (17: 17: 18: 19: 19), P6, patt 7 (7: 7: 9: 9: 9) sts, P6, patt 10 (10: 12: 13: 14: 16) sts.

Key

☐	K on RS, P on WS
⊡	P on RS, K on WS
◿▢▢◺	Cr4R
◺▢▢◿	Cr4L
▱▱	C6B
▱▱	C6F

Chart B

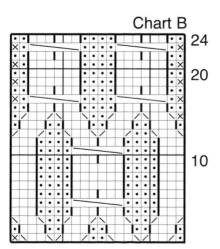

Chart A

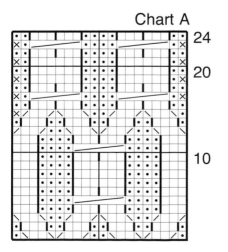

These 4 rows set the sts – 2 cables panels of 6 sts with sts between and at sides in textured patt, and front opening edge sts in ridge patt. Working cables on 5th (5th: 5th: 7th: next: next) and 1 (1: 1: 1: 2: 2) foll 8th rows as set by back, cont as folls:

L, XL and XXL sizes
Work – (-: -: 0: 2: 2) rows.
Next row (dec) (RS): Patt to marker, P2tog, patt to within 2 sts of next marker, P2tog tbl, patt to end. – (-: -: 50: 52: 54) sts.

All sizes
Work 6 (6: 6: 7: 7: 7) rows.
Next row (dec) (RS): Work 2 tog, patt to first marker, P2tog, patt to within 2 sts of next marker, P2tog tbl, patt to end.
43 (43: 45: 47: 49: 51) sts.
Work 5 rows.
Next row (dec) (RS): Patt to first marker, P2tog, patt to within 2 sts of next marker, P2tog tbl, patt to end. 41 (41: 43: 45: 47: 49) sts.
Work 3 rows.
Next row (dec) (RS): Work 2 tog, patt to marker, P3tog, patt to end.
38 (38: 40: 42: 44: 46) sts.
Work 3 rows.
Change to 6 ½mm (US 10 ½) needles.
Next row (RS): Patt to first marker, C6B, patt to next marker (this is just 1 st at this point), C6B, patt to end.
Work 5 rows.
Next row (RS): Patt to first marker, inc in st between this marker and next marker, patt to end. 39 (39: 41: 43: 45: 47) sts.
Next row: Patt to first marker, M1, K2, M1, patt to end. 41 (41: 43: 45: 47: 49) sts.
Remove markers.
Change to 7mm (US 10 ½/11) needles.
Now place chart as folls:
Row 1 (RS): Patt 6 (6: 8: 9: 10: 12) sts, work next 20 sts as row 1 of chart A, patt 17 (17: 17: 18: 19: 19) sts.
Row 2: Patt 17 (17: 17: 18: 19: 19) sts, work next 20 sts as row 2 of chart A, patt 6 (6: 8: 9: 10: 12) sts.
These 2 rows set the sts – cable panel with textured st either side and front opening edge sts still in ridge st.
Cont as set, shaping side seam by inc 1 st at beg of 3rd and 3 foll 8th rows, taking inc sts into textured patt. 45 (45: 47: 49: 51: 53) sts.
Work 5 (5: 7: 7: 7: 7) rows, ending with a WS row.
Shape armhole

Keeping patt correct, cast off 3 sts at beg of next row.
42 (42: 44: 46: 48: 50) sts.
Work 1 row.
Dec 1 st at armhole edge of next 3 (3: 5: 5: 5: 5) rows, then on foll 3 (3: 2: 3: 3: 4) alt rows. 36 (36: 37: 38: 40: 41) sts.
Cont straight until 8 (10: 12: 12: 12: 14) rows less have been worked than on back to beg of shoulder shaping, ending with a WS row.
Shape neck
Next row (RS): Patt 24 (25: 26: 26: 27: 28) sts and turn, leaving rem 12 (11: 11: 12: 13: 13) sts on a holder.
Keeping patt correct, dec 1 st at neck edge of next 2 rows, then on foll 2 (3: 4: 4: 4: 5) alt rows. 20 (20: 20: 20: 21: 21) sts.
Work 1 row, ending with a WS row.
Shape shoulder
Cast off 7 sts at beg of next row, then 7 (6: 7: 7: 7: 7) sts at beg of foll alt row.
Work 1 row.
Cast off rem 6 (7: 6: 6: 7: 7) sts.

RIGHT FRONT
Cast on 42 (42: 44: 46: 48: 50) sts using 7mm (US 10 ½/11) needles.
Row 1 (RS): P6 (6: 6: 7: 8: 8), (P1, K1 tbl) 5 rimes, P1, inc once in each of next 3 sts, P1, (K1 tbl, P1) 4 times, inc once in each of next 3 sts, (P1, K1 tbl) 5 (5: 6: 6: 7: 8) times, P0 (0: 0: 1: 0: 0).
48 (48: 50: 52: 54: 56) sts.
Row 2: K10 (10: 12: 13: 14: 16), wrap next st and turn.
Row 3: (P1, K1 tbl) 5 (5: 6: 6: 7: 8) times, P0 (0: 0: 1: 0: 0).
Row 4: K10 (10: 12: 13: 14: 16), P6, K9, wrap next st and turn.
Row 5: P1, (K1 tbl, P1) 4 times, K6, (P1, K1 tbl) 5 (5: 6: 6: 7: 8) times, P0 (0: 0: 1: 0: 0).
Row 6: K10 (10: 12: 13: 14: 16), P6, K9, P6, K17 (17: 17: 19: 21: 21).
Now work in patt as folls:
Row 1 (RS): K6 (6: 6: 7: 8: 8), P1, (K1 tbl, P1) 5 times, (C6B) 1 (1: 1: 0: 0: 0) times, K0 (0: 0: 6: 6: 6), place marker on needle, P1, (K1 tbl, P1) 4 times, place marker on needle, (C6B) 1 (1: 1: 0: 0: 0) times, K0 (0: 0: 6: 6: 6), (P1, K1 tbl) 5 (5: 6: 6: 7: 8) times, P0 (0: 0: 1: 0: 0). (2 markers in total.)
Taking markers up work, cont as folls:
 Row 2: K10 (10: 12: 13: 14: 16), P6, K9, P6,

K11, P6 (6: 6: 7: 8: 8).
These 2 rows set position of textured patt between markers and at side seam edge.
Keeping textured patt correct, cont as folls:
Row 3: P6 (6: 6: 7: 8: 8), P1, (K1 tbl, P1) 5 times, K6 (6: 6: 0: 6: 6), (C6B) 0 (0: 0: 1: 0: 0) times, (P2tog, patt 5 sts, P2tog tbl) 1 (1: 1: 0: 0: 0) times, patt 0 (0: 0: 9: 9: 9) sts, K6 (6: 6: 0: 6: 6), (C6B) 0 (0: 0: 1: 0: 0) times, patt 10 (10: 12: 13: 14: 16) sts. 46 (46: 48: 52: 54: 56) sts.
Row 4: Patt 10 (10: 12: 13: 14: 16) sts, P6, patt 7 (7: 7: 9: 9: 9) sts, P6, K17 (17: 17: 18: 19: 19).
These 4 rows set the sts – 2 cables panels of 6 sts with sts between and at sides in textured patt, and front opening edge sts in ridge patt. Working cables on 5th (5th: 5th: 7th: next: next) and 1 (1: 1: 1: 2: 2) foll 8th rows as set by back, cont as folls:

L, XL and XXL sizes
Work – (-: -: 0: 2: 2) rows.
Next row (dec) (RS): Patt to marker, P2tog, patt to within 2 sts of next marker, P2tog tbl, patt to end. – (-: -: 50: 52: 54) sts.

All sizes
Work 6 (6: 6: 7: 7: 7) rows.
Next row (dec) (RS): Patt to first marker, P2tog, patt to within 2 sts of next marker, P2tog tbl, patt to last 2 sts, work 2 tog.
43 (43: 45: 47: 49: 51) sts.
Work 5 rows.
Next row (dec) (RS): Patt to first marker, P2tog, patt to within 2 sts of next marker, P2tog tbl, patt to end.
41 (41: 43: 45: 47: 49) sts.
Work 3 rows.
Next row (dec) (RS): Patt to marker, P3tog, patt to last 2 sts, work 2 tog.
38 (38: 40: 42: 44: 46) sts.
Work 3 rows.
Change to 6 ½mm (US 10 ½) needles.
XS, S, M, XL and XXL sizes
Next row (RS): K2, K2tog tbl, yfwd (to make first buttonhole), patt to first marker, C6B, patt to next marker (this is just 1 st at this point), C6B, patt to end.
Working a further 4 buttonholes in this way on every foll 12th row and noting that no further reference will be made to buttonholes, cont as folls:
Work 5 rows.
L size
Next row (RS): Patt to first marker, C6B, patt

to next marker (this is just 1 st at this point), C6B, patt to end.

Work 1 row.

Next row (RS): K2, K2tog tbl, yfwd (to make first buttonhole), patt to end.

Working a further 4 buttonholes in this way on every foll 12th row and noting that no further reference will be made to buttonholes, cont as folls:

Work 3 rows.

All sizes

Next row (RS): Patt to first marker, inc in st between this marker and next marker, patt to end.

39 (39: 41: 43: 45: 47) sts.

Next row: Patt to first marker, M1, K2, M1, patt to end. 41 (41: 43: 45: 47: 49) sts.

Remove markers.

Change to 7mm (US 10 ½/11) needles.

Now place chart as folls:

Row 1 (RS): Patt 17 (17: 17: 18: 19: 19) sts, work next 20 sts as row 1 of chart B, patt 6 (6: 8: 9: 10: 12) sts.

Row 2: Patt (6: 8: 9: 10: 12) sts, work next 20 sts as row 2 of chart B, patt 17 (17: 17: 18: 19: 19) 6 sts.

These 2 rows set the sts – cable panel with textured st either side and front opening edge sts still in ridge st.

Keeping sts correct as set, complete to match left front, reversing shapings, and working first row of neck shaping as folls:

Shape neck

Next row (RS): Patt 12 (11: 11: 12: 13: 13) sts and slip these sts onto a holder, patt to end. 24 (25: 26: 26: 27: 28) sts.

SLEEVES (both alike)

Cast on 33 (35: 35: 37: 39: 41) sts using 7mm (US 10 ½/11) needles.

Row 1 (RS): P1, *K1 tbl, P1; rep from * to end.

Row 2: Knit.

These 2 rows form textured patt.

Cont in patt, shaping sides by inc 1 st at each end of 15th and 2 foll 16th rows, then on 2 foll 14th rows, taking inc sts into patt. 43 (45: 45: 47: 49: 51) sts.

Cont straight until sleeve measures 44 (45: 46: 47: 48: 49) cm, ending with a WS row.

Shape top

Keeping patt correct, cast off 3 sts at beg

of next 2 rows.

37 (39: 39: 41: 43: 45) sts.

Dec 1 st at each end of next and 3 (3: 3: 4: 4: 5) foll 4th rows, then on foll 3 (4: 4: 3: 4: 3) alt rows, then on foll 5 rows, ending with a WS row.

Cast off rem 13 (13: 13: 15: 15: 17) sts.

MAKING UP

Pin out the pieces and press carefully following instructions on ball band.

Join both shoulder seams using back stitch, or mattress stitch if preferred.

Collar

Using 6 ½mm (US 10 ½) needles and with RS facing, slip 12 (11: 11: 12: 13: 13) sts from right front holder onto right needle, rejoin yarn and pick up and knit 12 (14: 16: 16: 16: 18) sts up right side of neck, 19 (21: 23: 25: 27: 29) sts from back, and 12 (14: 16: 16: 16: 18) sts down left side of neck, then patt across 12 (11: 11: 12: 13: 13) sts on left front holder.

67 (71: 77: 81: 85: 91) sts.

Row 1 (WS of body): Patt 6 (6: 6: 7: 8: 8) sts, K to last 6 (6: 6: 7: 8: 8) sts, patt 6 (6: 6: 7: 8: 8) sts.

Row 2: Patt 6 (6: 6: 7: 8: 8) sts, P1, *K1 tbl, P1; rep from * to last 6 (6: 6: 7: 8: 8) sts, patt 6 (6: 6: 7: 8: 8) sts.

Last 2 rows set the sts.

Cont as set for a further 12 rows, ending with a **RS** row.

Cast off in patt (on **WS**).

Join side seams. Join sleeve seams. Set in sleeves. Sew on buttons.

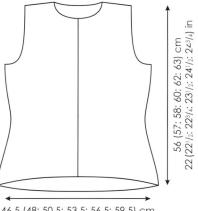

46.5 (48: 50.5: 53.5: 56.5: 59.5) cm
18¼ (19: 20: 21: 21¼: 23½) in

56 (57: 58: 60: 62: 63) cm
22 (22½: 22¾: 23½: 24½: 24¾) in

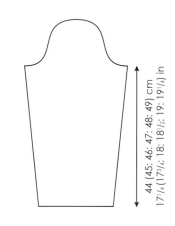

44 (45: 46: 47: 48: 49) cm
17¼ (17¾: 18: 18½: 19: 19¼) in

Recommendation

Suitable for the novice knitter.
Please see pages 20 & 23 for photographs.

	XS-S	M-L	XL-XXL	
To fit	**81-86**	**91-97**	**102-109**	cm
bust	32-34	36-38	40-43	in

Rowan Big Wool

	4	4	5	x100gm

Photographed in Commodore^K /Mulberry
^KKim Hargreaves for Rowan

Buttons – 2

Needles

1 pair 10mm (no 000) (US 15) needles
1 pair 12 mm (US 17) needles

Tension

8 sts and 11 rows to 10 cm measured over
stocking stitch using 12 mm (US 17) needles

BELLA
SHRUG WITH OVERSIZED COLLAR

BACK AND FRONTS (knitted in one piece)
Cast on 66 (76: 84) sts using 12 mm (US 17)
needles.
Row 1 (RS): K8 (9: 9) sts, (P2: K2) to last
6 (7: 7) sts, K6 (7: 7).
Row 2: K6 (7: 7), P2, (K2, P2) to last 6 (7: 7)
sts, K6 (7: 7) sts.
Repeat the last 2 rows twice more, ending
with a WS row.
Place markers on the needle, either side of
the 19th (22nd: 24th) st in from each end,
to indicate the side seam.
Note: Take the markers up the knitting by
slipping them from left to right needle on
every row.
Next row (RS): Knit.
Next row: K6 (7: 7), P to last 6 (7: 7) sts, K6
(7: 7).
The last 2 rows set the sts, i.e. 6 (7: 7) sts at
both ends worked in garter stitch and rem sts
worked in st st throughout.
Shape side seam
Next row (RS) (inc): K to 2 sts before first
marker, M1, K5, M1, K to 2 sts before second
marker, M1, K5, M1, K to end.70 (80: 88) sts.
Work 5 (7: 7) rows, ending with a WS row.
Inc as before on next row. 74 (84: 92) sts.
Work 5 (5: 7) rows, ending with a WS row.
Divide for armholes
Next row (RS): K19 (22: 24) sts for right
front, cast off next 3 sts, K until there are
30 (34: 38) sts on right needle for back, cast
off next 3 sts, K to end (19 (22: 24) sts), and
leaving stitches for right front and back on
holders, work left front as folls:
Left front
Dec 1 st at armhole edge on the next 2 (2: 3)
rows and 0 (1: 1) foll alt row, ending with a
RS (RS: WS) row. 17 (19: 20) sts.
Work 11 (11: 10) rows, ending with WS row.
Shape front neck
Next row (RS): K 10 (11: 11) sts and turn,
leaving rem 7 (8: 9) sts on a holder for collar.
Dec 1 st at neck edge on next 4 (4: 2) rows
and 0 (0: 2) foll alt rows. 6 (7: 7) sts.
Work 1 row, ending with a WS row.

Shape shoulder
Cast off 3 (4: 4) sts at beg of next row.
Work 1 row.
Cast off rem 3 sts.
Back
With **WS** facing rejoin yarn to stitches on
holder for back and work as folls:
Dec 1 st at each end of next 2 (2: 3) rows
and 0 (1: 1) foll alt row, ending with a
RS (RS: WS) row. 26 (28: 30) sts.
Work straight until back matches left front
to beg of shoulder shaping, ending with
a WS row.
Shape back neck and shoulders
Cast off 3 (4: 4) sts, K until 5 sts on right
needle and turn, leaving rem sts on a holder.
Work each side of neck separately.
Cast off 2 sts, work to end.
Cast off rem 3 sts.
With RS facing rejoin yarn to rem sts, cast
off centre 10 (10: 12) sts, K to end.
Complete to match first, side reversing
shaping.
Right front
With **WS** facing rejoin yarn to stitches on
holder for right front and work as folls:
Dec 1 st at armhole edge on next 2 (2: 3)
rows and 0 (1: 1) foll alt row, ending with
a RS (RS: WS) row. 17 (19: 20) sts.
Work 9 (9: 8) rows.
Next row (RS)(buttonhole): K2 (3: 3), K2tog,
yon, K to end.
Work 1 row.

42.5 (47.5: 52.5) cm
16³/₄ (18³/₄: 20³/₄) in

36 (40: 44) cm
14¹/₄ (15³/₄: 17¹/₄) in

Continued on opposite page...

SKYE

GENEROUS WRAP WORKED IN A TEXTURED STITCH

Recommendation
Suitable for the novice knitter.
Please see pages 4 & 38 for photographs.

Size
One size

Rowan Colourscape Chunky
4 x 100g
Photographed in Ghost

Needles
1 pair 8 mm (no 0) (US 11) needles

Tension
13 sts and 18 rows to 10 cm measured over textured stitch using 8mm (US 11mm) needles

Finished length
Approximately 48cm (19ins) wide and 188cm (74ins) long

Special abbreviations
K1b = K1 st though back loop

Pattern note:
The shades in **Colourscape** change continuously through the hank, starting and ending with slightly different colours. We have created the mirror image for this design by winding two of the four hanks from one end and two hanks from the other.

WRAP
Before starting your knitting, wind all four hanks of yarn into balls as folls: wind 2 balls starting from the same end and mark these 1 and 3, wind 2 balls from the opposite end and mark these 2 and 4.
Using ball 1, cast on 63 sts using 8mm (US 11mm) needles and work in pattern setting the stitches as folls:
Row 1 (RS): P10, (P1, K1b) to last 11 sts, P to end.
Row 2: Knit.
Row 3: K10, (P1, K1b) to last 11 sts, P1, K10.
Row 4: P10, K to last 10 sts, P10.
These 4 rows form the pattern and are repeated throughout.
Cont until the whole of the ball is used and then, working the balls in the order you have marked, cont until you have just enough yarn of the 4th ball left to cast off. Cast off.

Bella – Continued from previous page...

Shape front neck
Next row (RS): K7 (8: 9) sts and leave these on a holder for collar, K to end.
10 (11: 11) sts.
Complete as given for left front, reversing shaping.

MAKING UP
Press knitting using a warm iron over a damp cloth.
Join both shoulder seams using back stitch or mattress stitch if preferred.

Collar
With RS of right front facing and using 10 mm (US 15) needles needle, slip 7 (8: 9) stitches from holder on right front neck onto

right needle, rejoin yarn and pick up and knit 9 (11: 12) sts up right front neck, 18 (18: 22) sts across back and 9 (11: 12) sts down left front neck, K across 7 (8: 9) sts on holder.
50 (56: 64) sts.
With WS of garment and RS of collar (when folded over) facing, work as folls:
Row 1 (RS of collar): K8 (9: 9), (P2, K2) to last 6 (7: 7) sts, K to end.
Row 2: K6 (7: 7), (P2, K2) to last 8 (9: 9) sts, P2, K to end.
Work 3 rows, ending with a RS row.
Next row (WS) (buttonhole): K2 (3: 3), K2tog, yon, patt to end.
Work 3 more rows.
Change to 12 mm (US 17) needles.
Cont until collar measures 24 (25: 26) cm

from pick up row, ending with a RS row.
Cast off in patt.

Cap sleeves (both alike)
Cast on 40 (44: 48) sts using 10 mm (US 15) needles.
Row 1 (RS): K1, (P2, K2) to last 3 sts, P2, K1.
Row 2: P1, (K2, P2) to last 3 sts, K2, P1.
These 2 rows set the stitches.
Keeping rib correct, work 0 (1: 2) rows, ending with a WS (RS: WS) row.
Cast off 5 (6: 7) sts at beg of next 2 rows and then 5 sts at beg of foll 4 rows.
10 (12: 14) sts.
Cast off.
Join sleeve seams. Set sleeves into armholes. Sew on buttons.

BETH

A-LINE COAT IN DOUBLE MOSS STITCH

Recommendation

Suitable for the knitter with a little experience.
Please see pages 28 & 29 for photographs.

	XS	S	M	L	XL	XXL	
To fit	**81**	**86**	**91**	**97**	**102**	**109**	**cm**
bust	32	34	36	38	40	43	in

Rowan Big Wool

8 8 9 10 10 11 x 100gm
Photographed in Glum^K
^K Kim Hargreaves for Rowan

Buttons – 3 large & 2 medium

Needles

1 pair 10 mm (no 000) (US 15) needles
1 pair 12 mm (US 17) needles

Tension

9 sts and 12 rows to 10 cm measured over
double moss stitch using 12 mm (US 17)
needles

BACK

Cast on 49 (51: 53: 55: 57: 61) sts using
12 mm (US 17) needles.
Row 1 (RS): K0 (1: 0: 1: 0: 0), *P1, K1; rep from *
to last 1 (0: 1: 0: 1: 1) sts, P1 (0: 1: 0: 1: 1).
Row 2: P0 (1: 0: 1: 0: 0), *K1, P1; rep from *
to last 1 (0: 1: 0: 1: 1) sts, K1 (0: 1: 0: 1: 1).
Row 3: Work as row 2.
Row 4: Work as row 1.
These 4 rows form the pattern and are
repeated throughout.
Keeping patt correct, work a further 6 rows,
ending with a WS row.
Shape sides
Dec 1 st at each end of next row, then every foll
10th row until 39 (41: 43: 45: 47: 51) sts rem.
Cont straight until back measures 51 (51: 52:
52: 52: 52) cm, ending with a WS row.
Shape raglan armholes
Keeping patt correct, cast off 2 sts at beg of
next 2 rows. 35 (37: 39: 41: 43: 47) sts.
Dec 1 st at each end of next row and every
foll alt row to 15 (15: 17: 17: 21: 23) sts and
then on every foll row until 13 (13: 15: 15: 15:
17) sts rem. Cast off.

LEFT FRONT

Cast on 29 (30: 31: 32: 33: 35) sts using
12 mm (US 17) needles.
Row 1 (RS): K0 (1: 0: 1: 0: 0), *P1, K1; rep
from * to last 7 sts, P1, (K1, P1) 3 times.
Row 2: (P1, K1) 3 times, K1, *P1, K1; rep from *
to last 0 (1: 0: 1: 0: 0) sts, P0 (1: 0: 1: 0: 0).
Row 3: P0 (1: 0: 1: 0: 0), *K1, P1; rep from *
to last 7 sts, P1, (K1, P1) 3 times.
Row 4: (P1, K1) 3 times, K1, *K1, P1; rep from *
to last 0 (1: 0: 1: 0: 0) sts, K0 (1: 0: 1: 0: 0).
These 4 rows set the stitches, i.e. the main part
is worked in double moss st as for back, the 6
sts at centre front are worked in moss st, and
these are separated by 1 st worked in rev st st,
and are rep throughout. Keeping patt correct,
work a further 6 rows, ending with a WS row
Shape side
Dec 1 st at beg of next row, then every foll
10th row until 24 (25: 26: 27: 28: 30) sts rem.

Cont straight until left front matches back to
beg of raglan armhole shaping, ending with
a WS row.
Shape raglan armhole
Keeping patt correct, cast off 2 sts at beg
of next row. 22 (23: 24: 25: 26: 28) sts.
Work 1 row.
Dec 1 st at beg of next row and every foll alt
row until 18 (18: 19: 19: 20: 21) sts rem.
Work 1 row, ending with a WS row.
Shape front neck
Cont to dec at raglan edge on next row and
every foll alt row and **at the same time** shape
front neck as foll:
Next row (RS): Work to last 8 (8: 9: 9: 10: 11)
sts and turn, leaving rem sts on a holder for
neck edging.
Keeping raglan shaping correct, dec 1 st at
neck edge on next 4 rows and then on foll alt
row. 1 st. Fasten off.
Mark position of 2 buttons, the first to placed
18 rows below start of neck shaping, the
second 8 rows below start of neck shaping.

RIGHT FRONT

Cast on 29 (30: 31: 32: 33: 35) sts using
12 mm (US 17) needles.
Row 1 (RS): (P1, K1) 3 times, P1, *K1, P1;
rep from * to last 0 (1: 0: 1: 0: 0) sts, K0 (1:
0: 1: 0: 0) sts.
Row 2: P0 (1: 0: 1: 0: 0), *K1, P1; rep from *
to last 7 sts, K1, (K1, P1) 3 times.
Row 3: (P1, K1) 3 times, P1, *P1, K1; rep from *
to last 0 (1: 0: 1: 0: 0) sts, P0 (1: 0: 1: 0: 0).
Row 4: K0 (1: 0: 1: 0: 0), *P1, K1; rep from *
to last 7 sts, K1, (K1, P1) 3 times.
These 4 rows set the stitches and are rep
throughout.
Keeping patt correct, work a further 6 rows,
ending with a WS row.
Shape side
Dec 1 st at end of next row, then every foll
10th row until 24 (25: 26: 27: 28: 30) sts
rem and **at the same time** work buttonholes
to correspond with button markers on left
front and worked as folls:

Buttonhole row (RS): Patt 2, patt 2tog, yon, patt to end.

Cont straight until right front matches back to beg of raglan armhole shaping, ending with a WS row.

Shape raglan armhole

Work 1 row.

Next row (WS): Keeping patt correct, cast off 2 sts at beg of next row.

22 (23: 24: 25: 26: 28) sts.

Dec 1 st at end of next row and every foll alt row until 18 (18: 19: 19: 20: 21) sts rem.

Work 1 row, ending with a WS row.

Shape front neck

Cont dec at raglan edge on next and every foll alt row and **at the same time** shape front neck as folls:

Next row (RS): Work 8 (8: 9: 9: 10: 11) sts and leave these sts on a holder for neck edging, patt to end.

Keeping raglan shaping correct, dec 1 st at neck edge on next 4 rows and then on foll alt row. 1 st. Fasten off.

LEFT SLEEVE

Sleeve front

Cast on 25 (25: 27: 27: 27: 29) sts using 12 mm (US 17) needles.

Row 1 (RS): K1, (P1, K1) to end.

Row 2: P1, (K1, P1) to end.

Row 3: Work as row 2.

Row 4: Work as row 1.

These 4 rows form the pattern and are repeated throughout.

Cont in patt until 12 rows have been completed, ending with a WS row.

Break yarn and leave sts on a spare needle.

Sleeve back

Cast on 11 (11: 11: 11: 13: 13) sts using 12mm (US 17) needles, and work 12 rows in double moss st, setting stitches as given for sleeve front, and ending with a WS row.

Do not break yarn.

Join sleeve back and front

Working on sts for sleeve back, patt to last 5 sts, now holding sleeve back behind front and taking 1 st from each needle together, patt 5 sts, patt to end.

31 (31: 33: 33: 35: 37) sts.

Work 7 rows, ending with a WS row.

Dec 1 st at each end of next row and foll 20th row. 27 (27: 29: 29: 31: 33) sts.

Work straight until sleeve measures 44 (45: 46: 47: 48: 49) cm from cast on edge, ending with a WS row.

Shape raglan

Keeping patt correct cast off 2 sts at beg of next 2 rows. 23 (23: 25: 25: 27: 29) sts.

Work 2 rows.

Dec 1 st at each end of next row and 1 (2: 1: 3: 2: 3) foll 4th rows, and then on every foll alt row to 9 (9: 9: 11: 11: 13) sts, ending with a **RS** row. ***

Shape sleeve top

Next row (WS): Cast off 4 (4: 4: 5: 5: 6) sts, patt to end.

Next row: Patt 2 tog, patt to end.

Cast off rem 4 (4: 4: 5: 5: 6) sts.

RIGHT SLEEVE

Sleeve back

Cast on 11 (11: 11: 11: 13: 13) sts using 12mm (US 17) needles and work 12 rows in double moss st, setting stitches as given for left sleeve front, and ending with a WS row. Break yarn and leave sts on a spare needle.

Sleeve front

Cast on 25 (25: 27: 27: 27: 29) sts using 12 mm (US 17) needles and work 12 rows in double moss st, setting stitches as given for left sleeve front, and ending with a WS row.

Do not break yarn.

Join sleeve back and front

Working on sts for sleeve front, patt to last 5 sts, now holding sleeve back **behind** sleeve front and taking 1 st from each needle together, patt 5 sts, patt to end.

31 (31: 33: 33: 35: 37) sts.

Cont as given for left sleeve to ***.

Shape sleeve top

Work 1 row.

Next row (RS): Cast off 4 (4: 4: 5: 5: 6) sts, patt to last 2 sts, patt 2tog.

Next row: Patt to end.

Cast off rem 4 (4: 4: 5: 5: 6) sts

MAKING UP

Join raglan seams using backstitch or mattress stitch if preferred.

Neck edging

With RS of right front facing and using 12 mm (US 17) needles, slip 8 (8: 9: 9: 10: 11) sts from holder onto the right needle, pick up and knit 8 sts up right front neck, 7 (7: 7: 9: 9: 11) sts across right sleeve, 11 (11: 13:

13: 15: 15) sts across back neck, 7 (7: 7: 9: 9: 11) sts across left sleeve and 8 sts down left front, work in patt across 8 (8: 9: 9: 10: 11) sts on holder on left front.

57 (57: 61: 65: 69: 75) sts

Next row (WS): Work in moss st as set on front bands.

Next row (RS) (buttonhole): Patt 2, patt 2 tog, yon, patt to end.

Work 1 (1: 2: 2: 3: 3) rows.

Change to 10 mm (US 15) needles and work 3 more rows.

Cast off in pattern, and please note, to ensure that the edging fits neatly you will need to cast off quite firmly.

Join side and sleeve seams.

Sew the three larger buttons onto the left front.

Sew a smaller button onto each cuff, approximately 3cm from lower edge and through both layers of knitting.

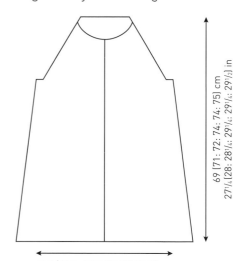

43.5 (45.5: 47.5: 50: 52: 56.5) cm
17¼ (18: 18¾: 19¾: 20½: 22¼) in

69 (71: 72: 74: 74: 75) cm
27¼ (28: 28¼: 29¼: 29¼: 29½) in

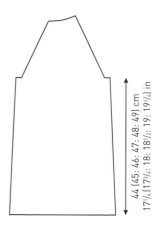

44 (45: 46: 47: 48: 49) cm
17¼ (17¾: 18: 18½: 19: 19¼) in

BLOOM

PRETTY BEADED SWEATER WITH LACE BUTTONED TRIM

Recommendation

Suitable for the knitter with a little experience.
Please see pages 34 & 35 for photographs.

	XS	S	M	L	XL	XXL	
To fit	**81**	**86**	**91**	**97**	**102**	**107**	cm
bust	32	34	36	38	40	42	in

Rowan Classic Cashsoft 4 ply

	8	8	9	9	10	11	x 50gm

Photographed in Folly ᴷ
ᴷ Kim Hargreaves for Rowan Classic

Buttons – 10

Beads – Approx 1350 (1400: 1450: 1500:
1550: 1600) x 0.8

Needles

1 pair 2 ¾ mm (no 12) (US 2) needles
1 pair 3mm (no 11) (US 2/3) needles
2.50 mm (US C2) crochet hook

Tension

28 sts and 39 rows to 10 cm measured over
beaded stocking stitch using 3 mm (US 2/3)
needles.

Special abbreviations

MP = Make picot: Cast-on 1 st, cast-off 1 st.
(See information page for details)
Cluster 2 = Bring a bead up to knitting, yrn,
P2, holding the bead to the front of the work,
lift the yrn over last 2 sts and off RH needle.

BACK

Lower back edging

Cast on 24 sts using 2 ¾ mm (US 2) needles
and work as folls:
Row 1 (RS): MP, P to end.
Row 2: Knit.
Row 3: MP, K to end.
Row 4: P1, *P2tog, yrn; rep from * to last st, P1.
Row 5: MP, P to end.
Row 6: Knit.
Row 7: MP, K to end.
Row 8: Purl.
Rep last 8 rows a further 18 (19: 21: 23: 24: 26)
times, then rows 1 – 6 again, end with a WS row.
Cast off, but do not break yarn.

Upper back

With RS facing and using 3 mm (US 2/3)
needles, pick up and knit 102 (110: 116:
124: 132: 140) sts along top (straight edge)
of border and turn, **purl** to end.
Cont in patt from chart for back, rep the
12 row patt throughout, and **at the same
time,** work shaping as folls:
Chart rows 1 & 3 (RS): Knit.
Chart 2: Purl.
Break yarn and thread on the beads (don't be
tempted to thread too many because the yarn
will get very heavy).
Chart row 4 (WS): P5 (3: 6: 4: 2: 6), * cluster
2, P4; rep from * to last 7 (5: 8: 6: 4: 8) sts,
cluster 2, P5 (3: 6: 4: 6).
Chart row 5: Knit.
Chart row 6: Purl.
Chart row 7: K2tog, K to last 2 sts, K2tog.
100 (108: 114: 122: 130: 138) sts.
Cont until chart row 12 completed, dec 1 st
as before at each end of chart row 11 and
ending with a WS row.
98 (106: 112: 120: 128: 136) sts.
Cont in patt shaping sides as folls:
Work 2 rows.
Dec 1 st as before at each end of next row
and 2 foll 4th rows.
92 (100: 106: 114: 122: 130) sts.
Work 15 (15: 17: 17: 17: 17) rows, ending
with a WS row.

Inc 1 st at each end of next row and every foll
8th row to 110 (118: 124: 132: 140: 148) sts.
Work straight until back measures 29 (29:
30: 30: 30: 30) cm from top of lower edging,
ending with a WS row.

Shape armholes

Cast off 5 (5: 7: 7: 7: 7) sts at beg of next
2 rows.
100 (108: 110: 118: 126: 134) sts.
Dec 1 st at each end of next 5 (7: 7: 9: 9: 9)
rows, then on 2 (2: 1: 1: 2: 3) foll alt rows,
and then on foll 4th row, ending with a **RS**
row. 84 (88: 92: 96: 102: 108) sts. ***
Work straight until armhole measures 17 (18:
18: 19: 20: 21) cm, ending with a WS row.

Shape shoulders and back neck

Cast off 8 (8: 9: 9: 9: 10) sts at beg of next
2 rows.
Cast off 7 (8: 8: 8: 9: 10) sts, patt until
11 (11: 11: 12: 13: 13) sts on right needle
and turn, leaving rem sts on a holder.
Work each side of neck separately.
Cast off 4 sts, work to end.
Cast off rem 7 (7: 7: 8: 9: 9) sts.
With RS facing rejoin yarn to rem sts, cast off
centre 32 (34: 36: 38: 40: 42) sts, work to end.
Complete to match first side, rev shaping.
Place a marker at each end of the 40th
(42nd: 44th: 46th: 48th: 50th) row down
from beg of shoulder shaping. These markers
indicate where the shaped shoulder sections
on the upper front start.

FRONT

Main section

Work as given for back to ***.
Next row (WS): Cast off purlwise.
Shoulder sections
Left front shoulder
Thread approximately 20 beads onto yarn.
Cast on 1 st using 3 mm (US 2/3) needles,
cont in st st shaping as folls and **at the same
time,** place beads as before to match beads
on left side of back from marker upwards.
Next row (RS) (inc): Knit into back and front
of st. 2sts.

Next row: Purl.

Cont to inc 1 st at end of next row and every foll alt row until 20 (21: 22: 23: 24: 25) sts on needle, ending with a **RS** row.

Work 1 row, inc 1 st at beg of row on **XXL size only.**

20 (21: 22: 23: 24: 26) sts.

Shape shoulder

XS, S, M & L sizes only:

Cast off 8 (8: 8: 9) sts at beg and inc 1 st at end of next row.

13 (14: 15: 15) sts.

Work 1 row.

Cast off 7 (8: 8: 8) sts at beg and inc 1 st at end of next row.

7 (7: 8: 8) sts.

Work 1 row.

Cast off.

XL & XXL sizes only:

Cast off 9 (10) sts at beg and inc 1 st at end of next row.

16 (17) sts.

Inc 1 st, work to end. 17 (18) sts.

Cast off 9 (10) sts at beg of next and inc 1 st at end of next row. 9 sts.

Work 1 row.

Cast off.

Right front shoulder

Thread approximately 20 beads onto yarn.

Cast on 1 st using 3 mm (US 2/3) needles, cont in st st shaping as folls and **at the same time,** place beads as before to match beads on right side of back from marker upwards.

Next row (RS) (inc): Knit into back and front of st. 2sts.

Next row: Purl.

Cont to inc 1 st at beg of next row and every foll alt row until 20 (21: 22: 23: 24: 25) sts on needle, ending with a RS row.

Work 1 row, inc 1 st at end of row on **XXL size only.** 20 (21: 22: 23: 24: 26) sts.

Shape shoulder

Work 1 row, ending with a **RS** row.

XS, S, M & L sizes only:

Cast off 8 (8: 8: 9) sts at beg and inc 1 st at end of next row.

13 (14: 15: 15) sts.

Work 1 row.

Cast off 7 (8: 8: 8) sts at beg and inc 1 st at end of next row. 7 (7: 8: 8) sts.

Work 1 row. Cast off.

XL & XXL sizes only:

Cast off 9 (10) sts at beg and inc 1 st at end of next row. 16 (17) sts.

Inc 1 st, work to end. 17 (18) sts.

Cast off 9 (10) sts at beg of next and inc 1 st at end of next row. 9 sts.

Work 1 row.

Cast off. (as above)

SLEEVES (work 2)

Lower edging (worked in 2 pieces)

Cast on 16 sts using 2 ¾ mm (US 2) needles and work as folls:

Row 1 (RS): MP, P to end.

Row 2: Knit.

Row 3: MP, K to end.

Row 4: P1, *P2tog, yrn; rep from * to last st, P1.

Row 5: MP, P to end.

Row 6: Knit.

Row 7: MP, K to end.

Row 8: Purl.

Rep last 8 rows a further 10 (11: 11: 11: 12: 12), then rows 1 – 6 again, ending with a WS row.

Cast off but do not break the yarn.

With RS facing and using 3 mm (US 2/3) needles, pick up and knit 62 (66: 68: 70: 74: 76) sts along top (straight edge) of border and turn, **purl** to end.

Break yarn and thread beads.

Cont in patt from chart, working between the appropriate markers, rep the 12 row patt throughout, and **at the same time,** work shaping as folls:

Work 4 rows from chart, ending with a WS row.

Keeping patt correct, inc 1 st at each end of next row. 64 (68: 70: 72: 76: 78) sts.

Work 17 rows, ending with a WS row.

Inc 1 st at each end of next row and 6 (6: 6: 6: 1: 1) foll 18th rows, and then for **XL & XXL sizes only,** 5 foll 20th rows.

78 (82: 84: 86: 90: 92) sts.

Cont until sleeve measures 36 (37: 38: 39: 40: 41) cm from top of lower edging, ending with a WS row.

Shape top

Cast off 5 (5: 7: 7: 7: 7) sts at beg of next 2 rows.

68 (72: 70: 72: 76: 78) sts.

Dec 1 st at each end of the next 2 (2: 0: 0: 0: 0) rows.

64 (68: 70: 72: 76: 78) sts.

Dec 1 st at each end of next row and foll alt row. Work 3 rows.

Dec 1 st at each end of next row and every foll 4th row to 48 (52: 52: 52: 56: 54) sts, ending with a **RS** row.

Work 1 row.

Chart for back, front & sleeve ☐ K on RS, P on WS ⊠ cluster 2

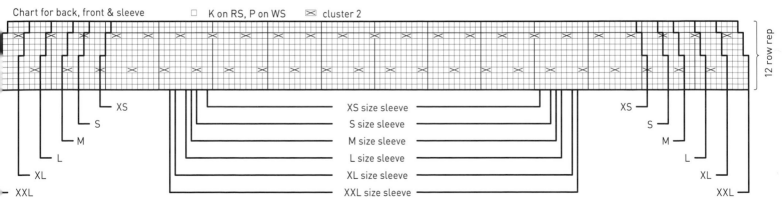

12 row rep

XS

S

M

L

XL

XXL

XS size sleeve
S size sleeve
M size sleeve
L size sleeve
XL size sleeve
XXL size sleeve

XS
S
M
L
XL
XXL

Dec 1 st at each end of next row and 3 (5: 4: 4: 5: 2) foll alt rows, and then on every foll row to 30 (30: 32: 32: 34: 34) sts.
Cast off 4 sts at beg of next 2 rows.
Cast off rem 22 (22: 24: 24: 26: 26) sts.

MAKING UP

Press all pieces using a warm iron over a damp cloth.

Join the front shoulder sections to the back along the shoulder seams using back stitch or mattress st if preferred.

Front and back neck edging

With RS facing and using 2 ¾ mm (US 2) needles pick up and knit 40 (42: 44: 46: 48: 50) sts along shaped side of right front shoulder section, 40 (42: 44: 46: 48: 50) sts across back neck and 40 (42: 44: 46: 48: 50) sts along shaped edge of left front shoulder section.

120 (126: 132: 138: 144: 150) sts.

Next row (WS): K1 (0: 1: 0: 1: 0) sts, (P2, K2) to last 3 (2: 3: 2: 3: 2) sts, K3 (2: 3: 2: 3: 2).

This row sets the sts for (K2, K2) rib.

Keeping rib patt correct, inc 1 st at each end of next 11 rws, ending with a **RS** row.

Cast off in patt.

Lower front neck edging

With RS facing and using 2 ¾ mm (US 2) needles pick up and knit 84 (88: 92: 96: 102: 108) sts across top edge of lower front and work in K2, P2 rib setting sts as folls:

Next row (WS): K1 (1: 1: 1: 0: 1) sts, (K2, P2) to last 3 (3: 3: 3: 2: 3) sts, K3 (3: 3: 3: 2: 3).

Next row: K1 (1: 1: 1: 0: 1) sts, (P2, K2) to last 3 (3: 3: 3: 2: 3) sts, P2, K1 (1: 1: 1: 0: 1).

Rep these last 2 rows 5 times more, ending with a **RS** row.

Cast off in patt.

Place the back on a flat surface WS uppermost, with WS facing place the lower front on top of back carefully matching the armholes. Fold the upper front sections onto the lower front so that the ribs overlap and sew together securely at the side edge.

Join side and sleeve seams, leaving side seams open at border edges.

Set sleeve into armhole.

Using a 2.50 mm (US C2) crochet hook, make 5 button loops along each side of front border edge. Sew on buttons to correspond with button loops.

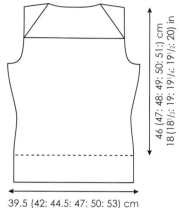

46 (47: 48: 49: 50: 51:) cm
18 (18¹/₂: 19: 19¹/₄: 19¹/₂: 20) in

39.5 (42: 44.5: 47: 50: 53) cm
15¹/₂ (16¹/₂: 17¹/₂: 18¹/₂: 19¹/₂: 21) in

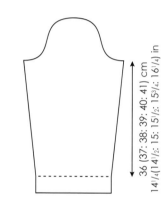

36 (37: 38: 39: 40: 41) cm
14¹/₄ (14¹/₂: 15: 15¹/₂: 15³/₄: 16¹/₄) in

GINNY

Recommendation

Suitable for the knitter with a little experience.
Please see pages 43, 45 & 47 for photographs.

	XS	S	M	L	XL	XXL	
To fit	**81**	**86**	**91**	**97**	**102**	**107**	cm
bust	32	34	36	38	40	42	in

Rowan Felted Tweed

| | 6 | 7 | 7 | 8 | 8 | 9 | x 50gm |

Photographed in Paisley[K]

[K] Kim Hargreaves for Rowan

Buttons – 6
Needles

1 pair 3mm (no 11) (US 2/3) needles
1 pair 3 ¼mm (no 10) (US 3) needles
1 pair 3 ¾mm (no 9) (US 5) needles

Tension

23 sts and 32 rows to 10 cm over stocking
stitch using 3 ¾mm (US 5) needles, 25 sts
and 34 rows to 10 cm over double moss st
using 3 ¾mm (US 5) needles.

BACK

Cast on 99 (105: 111: 117: 123: 131) sts
using 3 ¾ mm (US 5) needles.
Row 1 (RS): P1 (0: 1: 0: 1: 1), *K1, P1; rep
from * to last 0 (1: 0: 1: 0: 0) st, K0 (1: 0: 1:
0: 0).
Row 2: As row 1.
Rows 3 and 4: K1 (0: 1: 0: 1: 1), *P1, K1; rep
from * to last 0 (1: 0: 1: 0: 0) st, P0 (1: 0: 1:
0: 0).
These 4 rows form double moss st.
Cont in double moss st for a further 12 rows,
ending with a WS row.
Counting in from both ends of last row,
place markers on 26th (26th: 29th: 29th:
32nd: 32nd) sts in from ends of row.
Row 17 (dec) (RS): Work 2 tog, patt to within
1 st of marked st, work 3 tog, patt to within
1 st of next marker, work 3 tog tbl, patt to
last 2 sts, work 2 tog.
93 (99: 105: 111: 117: 125) sts.
Work 7 (7: 7: 9: 9: 9) rows.
Rep last 8 (8: 8: 10: 10: 10) rows twice more,
then row 17 again.
75 (81: 87: 93: 99: 107) sts.
Work 1 (3: 3: 3: 3: 5) rows, ending with
a WS row.
Change to 3mm (US 2/3) needles.
Now work in ridge patt as folls:
Row 1 (RS): Knit.
Row 2: Knit.
Rows 3 and 4: Purl.
These 4 rows form ridge patt.
Work in ridge patt for a further 16 (16:
16: 20: 20: 20) rows, ending with a
WS row.
Change to 3 ¾mm (US 5) needles.
Next row (inc) (RS): K3, M1, K to last 3 sts,
M1, K3.
Working all increases as set by last row and
beg with a P row, work in st st, shaping side
seams by inc 1 st at each end of 6th and
7 foll 6th rows.
93 (99: 105: 111: 117: 125) sts.
Work 7 (9: 11: 11: 11: 11) rows, ending with
a WS row.

Shape armholes

Cast off 5 sts at beg of next 2 rows.
83 (89: 95: 101: 107: 115) sts.
Dec 1 st at each end of next 3 (3: 3: 5: 5: 7)
rows, then on foll 3 (4: 5: 4: 5: 5) alt rows,
then on foll 4th row. 69 (73: 77: 81: 85: 89) sts.
Work 21 (17: 11: 11: 9: 7) rows, ending with
a WS row.
Beg with patt row 1, work in ridge patt for 24 (26:
30: 32: 36: 40) rows, ending with a WS row.

Shape shoulders and back neck

Cast off 7 (7: 7: 8: 8: 8) sts at beg of next 2 rows.
55 (59: 63: 65: 69: 73) sts.
Next row (RS): Cast off 6 (7: 7: 7: 7: 8) sts,
patt until there are 10 (10: 11: 11: 12: 12) sts
on right needle and turn, leaving rem sts on
a holder.
Work each side of neck separately.
Cast off 4 sts at beg of next row.
Cast off rem 6 (6: 7: 7: 8: 8) sts.
With RS facing rejoin yarn to rem sts, cast
off centre 23 (25: 27: 29: 31: 33) sts, patt to
end. Complete to match first side, reversing
shapings.

LEFT FRONT

Cast on 54 (57: 60: 63: 66: 70) sts using
3 ¾ mm (US 5) needles.
Row 1 (RS): P0 (1: 0: 1: 0: 0), *P1, K1; rep
from * to end.
Row 2: *K1, P1; rep from * to last 0 (1: 0:
1: 0: 0) st, K0 (1: 0: 1: 0: 0).
Row 3: K0 (1: 0: 1: 0: 0), *P1, K1; rep
from * to end.
Row 4: *P1, K1; rep from * to last 0 (1: 0:
1: 0: 0) st, P0 (1: 0: 1: 0: 0).
These 4 rows form double moss st.
Cont in double moss st for a further 12 rows,
ending with a WS row.
Counting in from end of last row, place
marker on 26th (26th: 29th: 29th:
32nd: 32nd) sts in from end of row.
Row 17 (dec) (RS): Work 2 tog, patt to within
1 st of marked st, work 3 tog, patt to end.
51 (54: 57: 60: 63: 67) sts.
Work 7 (7: 7: 9: 9: 9) rows.

Rep last 8 (8: 8: 10: 10: 10) rows twice more, then row 17 again.

42 (45: 48: 51: 54: 58) sts.

Work 1 (3: 3: 3: 3: 5) rows, ending with a WS row.

Change to 3mm (US 2/3) needles.

Work in ridge patt as given for back for 20 (20: 20: 24: 24: 24) rows, ending with a WS row.

Change to 3 ¾mm (US 5) needles.

Next row (inc) (RS): K3, M1, K to last 8 sts, (P1, K1) 4 times.

Next row: (K1, P1) 3 times, K2, P to end.

Next row: K to last 8 sts, P2, (K1, P1) 3 times.

Next row: (P1, K1) 4 times, P to end.

These 4 rows set the sts and side seam increases as given for back.

Cont as set, inc 1 st at beg of 3rd and 3 foll 6th rows.

47 (50: 53: 56: 59: 63) sts.

Work 5 rows, ending with a WS row.

Shape front slope

Next row (RS): K3, M1 (for side seam inc), K to last 10 sts, K2tog tbl (for front slope dec), patt to end.

Working all front slope decreases as set by last row, dec 1 st at front slope edge on 20th row and **at same time** inc 1 st at side seam edge of 6th and 2 foll 6th rows.

49 (52: 55: 58: 61: 65) sts.

Work 5 (7: 9: 9: 9: 9) rows, ending with a WS row.

Shape armhole

Keeping patt correct, cast off 5 sts at beg of next row.

44 (47: 50: 53: 56: 60) sts.

Work 1 row.

Dec 1 st at armhole edge of next 3 (3: 3: 5: 5: 7) rows, then on foll 3 (4: 5: 4: 5: 5) alt rows, then on foll 4th row and **at same time** dec 1 st at front slope edge on 13th (11th: 9th: 7th: 7th: 7th) row.

36 (38: 40: 42: 44: 46) sts.

Work 21 (17: 11: 11: 9: 7) rows, dec 1 st at front slope edge of 20th (16th: 10th: 10th: 8th: 6th) of these rows and ending with a WS row.

35 (37: 39: 41: 43: 45) sts.

Next row (RS): K8 (8: 8: 9: 9: 9), (K2tog) 6 (7: 8: 8: 9: 10) times, K7 (7: 7: 8: 8: 8), patt 8 sts.

29 (30: 31: 33: 34: 35) sts.

Next row: Patt 8 sts, K to end.

Next row: P to last 8 sts, patt to end.

Next row: Patt 8 sts, P to end.

Next row: K to last 8 sts, patt to end.

Last 4 rows set the sts – front opening edge 8 sts still in patt with all other sts now in ridge patt.

Cont as set, dec 1 st as before at front slope edge of 4th and 1 (1: 1: 2: 2: 2) foll 10th rows.

27 (28: 29: 30: 31: 32) sts.

Cont straight until left front matches back to beg of shoulder shaping, ending with a WS row.

Shape shoulder

Cast off 7 (7: 7: 8: 8: 8) sts at beg of next row, 6 (7: 7: 7: 7: 8) sts at beg of foll alt row, then 6 (6: 7: 7: 8: 8) sts at beg of foll alt row.

8 sts.

Cont in patt on these 8 sts only (for back neck border extension) for a further 6.5 (7: 7.5: 8: 8.5: 9) cm, ending with a WS row.

Cast off.

Mark positions for 6 buttons along left front opening edge – first to come in row 19, 3rd to come in 3rd row of waist ridge patt, 2nd to come midway between first and 3rd buttons, 4th to come in 17th (17th: 17th: 21st: 21st: 21st) row of waist ridge patt, 6th to come 1.5 cm below start of front slope shaping, and 5th button to come midway between 4th and 6th buttons.

RIGHT FRONT

Cast on 54 (57: 60: 63: 66: 70) sts using 3 ¾ mm (US 5) needles.

Row 1 (RS): *K1, P1; rep from * to last 0 (1: 0: 1: 0: 0) st, K0 (1: 0: 1: 0: 0).

Row 2: P0 (1: 0: 1: 0: 0), *P1, K1; rep from * to end.

Row 3: *P1, K1; rep from * to last 0 (1: 0: 1: 0: 0) st, P0 (1: 0: 1: 0: 0).

Row 4: K0 (1: 0: 1: 0: 0), *P1, K1; rep from * to end.

These 4 rows form double moss st.

Cont in double moss st for a further 12 rows, ending with a WS row.

Counting in from beg of last row, place marker on 26th (26th: 29th: 29th: 32nd: 32nd) sts in from end of row.

Row 17 (dec) (RS): Patt to within 1 st of marked st, work 3 tog tbl, patt to last 2 sts, work 2 tog.

51 (54: 57: 60: 63: 67) sts.

Work 1 row.

Row 19 (buttonhole row) (RS): Patt 3 sts, work 2 tog, yrn (to make a buttonhole), patt to end.

Working a further 5 buttonholes in this way to correspond with positions marked for buttons on left front and noting that no further reference will be made to buttonholes, cont as folls:

Work 5 (5: 5: 7: 7: 7) rows.

Working decreases as set by row 17, dec 3 sts across next and 2 foll 8th (8th: 8th: 10th: 10th: 10th) rows.

42 (45: 48: 51: 54: 58) sts.

Work 1 (3: 3: 3: 3: 5) rows, ending with a WS row.

Change to 3mm (US 2/3) needles.

Work in ridge patt as given for back for 20 (20: 20: 24: 24: 24) rows, ending with a WS row.

Change to 3 ¾mm (US 5) needles.

Next row (inc) (RS): (K1, P1) 4 times, K to last 3 sts, M1, K3.

Next row: P to last 8 sts, K2, (P1, K1) 3 times.

Next row: (P1, K1) 3 times, P2, K to end.

Next row: P to last 8 sts, (K1, P1) 4 times.

These 4 rows set the sts and side seam increases as given for back.

Cont as set, inc 1 st at end of 3rd and 3 foll 6th rows. 47 (50: 53: 56: 59: 63) sts.

Work 5 rows, ending with a WS row.

Shape front slope

Next row (RS): Patt 8 sts, K2tog (for front slope dec), K to last 3 sts, M1 (for side seam inc), K3.

Working all front slope decreases as set by last row, complete to match left front, reversing shapings.

SLEEVES (both alike)

Cast on 95 (97: 99: 101: 103: 105) sts using 3 ¾mm (US 5) needles.

Beg with a K row, work in st st for 6 rows, ending with a WS row.

Next row (RS)(dec): K2, K2tog, K to last 4 sts, K2tog tbl, K2.

Working all decreases as set by last row, dec 1 st at each end of 6th and 7 foll 6th rows, then on 12th row, then on 14th row, then on 20th row.

71 (73: 75: 77: 79: 81) sts.

Cont straight until sleeve measures 41 (42: 43: 44: 45: 46) cm from cast-on edge, ending with a WS row.

Shape top

Cast off 5 sts at beg of next 2 rows.
61 (63: 65: 67: 69: 71) sts.
Dec 1 st at each end of next 3 rows, then
on foll alt row, then on 6 (6: 6: 7: 8: 8) foll
4th rows, then on foll 2 (3: 3: 3: 3: 4) alt rows,
then on foll 5 rows, ending with a WS row.
29 (29: 31: 31: 31: 31) sts.
Cast off 3 sts at beg of next 2 rows.
Cast off rem 23 (23: 25: 25: 25: 25) sts.

Cuffs (both alike)

Cast on 24 (24: 24: 26: 26: 26) sts using
3mm (US 2/3) needles.
Row 1 (RS): Knit.
Rows 2 and 3: Purl.
Row 4 (WS): K7, wrap next st (by slipping next
st from left needle to right needle, taking yarn
to opposite side of work between needles and
then slipping same st back onto left needle –
when working back across wrapped sts, work
the wrapped st and the wrapping loop tog as
1 st) and turn.
Row 5: Knit.
Row 6: P14, wrap next st and turn.
Row 7: Purl.
Row 8: Knit.
Last 8 rows set position of ridge patt.
Cont in ridge patt for a further 63 (63: 63:
67: 67: 67) rows, ending with a RS P row.
Next row (WS): K14, wrap next st and turn.
Next row: Knit.
Next row: P7, wrap next st and turn.
Next row: Purl.
Work 3 rows.
Cast off.

MAKING UP

Pin out the pieces and press carefully
following instructions on ball band.
Join both shoulder seams using back stitch,
or mattress stitch if preferred. Join cast-off
ends of back neck border extensions, then
sew one row-end edge in place to back neck
edge. Join side seams.
Gathering cast-on edge of sleeve to fit, sew
sleeve to longer row-end edge of cuff.
Join sleeve and cuff seams. Set in sleeves.
Sew on buttons.

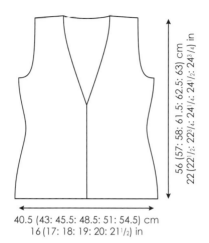

56 (57: 58: 61.5: 62.5: 63) cm
22 (22½: 22¾: 24¼: 24½: 24¾) in

40.5 (43: 45.5: 48.5: 51: 54.5) cm
16 (17: 18: 19: 20: 21½) in

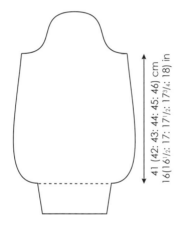

41 (42: 43: 44: 45: 46) cm
16 (16½: 17: 17½: 17¾: 18) in

ETHEREAL

WRAP-OVER CARDIGAN WITH SOFT COLLAR

Recommendation

Suitable for the knitter with a little experience.
Please see pages 37 & 52 for photographs.

	XS	S	M	L	XL	XXL	
To fit	**81**	**86**	**91**	**97**	**102**	**107**	**cm**
bust	32	34	36	38	40	42	in

Rowan Kidsilk Haze

| | 5 | 6 | 6 | 6 | 7 | 7 | x25gm |

Photographed in Trance

Buttons – 2

Needles

1 pair 2¼ mm (no 13) (US 1) needles
1 pair 2¾mm (no 12) (US 2) needles
1 pair 3¼ mm (no 10) (US 3) needles
2.50mm (US C2) crochet hook
1 pair 2¾ mm (no 12) (US 2) double-pointed
needles

Tension

25 sts and 34 rows to 10 cm measured over
pattern using 3¼ mm (US 3) needles.

Special abbreviations

MP = Make picot: cast on 1 st, cast off 1 st.
(See information page for details)
YO = yarn over (making 1 stitch)

Pattern note: because it is quite easy to cast
on too tightly with Kidsilk Haze we have used
a double cast-on, where twice the number of
stitches are cast on and then 2 sts worked
together across the first row.

BACK

Cast on 204 (216: 228: 240: 252: 272) sts
using 2¾ mm (US 2) needles and work as folls:
Row 1 (dec) (RS): (Sl1, P1, psso) to end.
102 (108: 114: 120: 126: 136) sts.
Row 2: Knit.
Row 3: Knit.
Row 4: Purl.
Row 5: Purl.
Row 6: Knit.
The last 4 rows form the horizontal rib pattern.
Work 4 (6: 6: 6: 6: 6) more rows in horizontal
rib, ending with a WS row.
Next row (RS) (dec): Keeping patt correct, work
2, work 2tog, work to last 4 sts, work 2tog tbl,
work 2. 100 (106: 112: 118: 124: 134) sts.
Work 3 (1: 1: 1: 1: 1) rows, ending with a WS row.
Change to 3¼ mm (US 3) needles and beg
with a K row, cont in in st st as folls:
Work 2 (4: 6: 8: 8) rows.
Next row (RS) (dec): K2, K2tog, K to last 4 sts,
K2tog tbl, K2. 98 (104: 110: 116: 122: 132) sts.
Work 5 (5: 5: 7: 7: 7) rows.
Dec 1 st as before at each end of next row
and 5 (5: 5: 5: 5: 1) foll 6th (6th: 6th: 6th:
6th: 8th) rows and then, for **XXL size only,**
on 4 foll 6th rows.
86 (92: 98: 104: 110: 120) sts.
Work 19 rows, ending with a WS row.
Next row (RS) (inc): K2, M1, K to last 2 sts,
M1, K2. 88 (94: 100: 106: 112: 122) sts.
Work 9 rows.
Inc as before at each end of next row and
3 (2: 2: 2: 1: 0) foll 10th rows and then on
0 (1: 1: 1: 2: 3) foll 8th rows.
96 (102: 108: 114: 120: 130) sts.
Work 9 (9: 11: 9: 9: 9) rows, ending with a WS row.
(Work should measure approx 36 (36: 37: 37:
37: 37) cm.)

Shape armholes

Cast off 5 sts at beg of next 2 rows.
86 (92: 98: 104: 110: 120) sts.
Dec 1 st at each end of next 3 (3: 3: 3: 3: 5)
rows, 2 (3: 3: 4: 5: 5) foll alt rows, and then
on 1 (1: 2: 2: 2: 3) foll 4th rows.
74 (78: 82: 86: 90: 94) sts.

Cont straight until back measures 17.5 (18.5:
18.5: 19.5: 20.5: 21.5) cm from beg of
armhole shaping, ending with a WS row.

Shape shoulders and back neck

Next row (RS): Knit 21 (22: 24: 25: 26: 27)
sts and turn, leaving rem sts on a holder.
Dec 1 st at beg of next row, P to end.
Cast off 6 (6: 7: 7: 8: 8) sts at beg and dec
1 st at end of next row.
Work last 2 rows once more.
Work 1 row.
Cast off rem 5 (6: 6: 7: 6: 7) sts.
With RS facing rejoin yarn to rem sts, cast
off centre 32 (34: 34: 36: 38: 40) sts,
K to end.
Complete to match first side, reversing
shaping.

LEFT FRONT

Cast on 168 (180: 188: 196: 206: 218) sts
using 2¾ mm (US 2) needles and work
as folls:
Row 1 (RS) (dec): (Sl1, P1, psso) to end.
84 (90: 94: 98: 103: 109) sts.
Row 2: MP, K to end.
**(Note that a picot is worked at the beg of
every WS row along the entire left front
opening edge.)**
Row 3: K to last 17 (17: 18: 18: 19: 19) sts,
yon, K2tog tbl, K15 (15: 16: 16: 17: 17) sts.
Row 4: MP, P to end.
Row 5: P to last 17 (17: 18: 18: 19: 19) sts,
yon, K2tog tbl, P15 (15: 16: 16: 17: 17) sts.
Row 6: MP, K to end.
The last 4 rows form the horizontal rib and
set the stitches for the front edging.
Work 4 (6: 6: 6: 6: 6) more rows in horizontal
rib, placing eyelets as before and ending with
a WS row.
Next row (RS) (dec): Keeping patt correct,
work 2, work 2tog, work to end.
83 (89: 93: 97: 102: 108) sts.
Work 3 (1: 1: 1: 1: 1) rows, ending with
a WS row.
All sizes
Change to 3¼ mm (US 3) needles.

Next row (RS): K to last 17 (17: 18: 18: 19: 19) sts, patt to end.

Next row: Patt 15 (15: 16: 16: 17: 17) sts, P to end.

These last 2 rows set the stitches.

Cont rep these 2 rows, working 17 (17: 18: 18: 19: 19) sts at front edge as set and rem sts in st st, and **at the same time** cont shaping side as folls:

Work 0 (2: 4: 4: 6: 6) rows, ending with a WS row.

Next row (RS) (dec): K2, K2tog, K to last 17 (17: 18: 18: 19: 19) sts, patt to end. 82 (88: 92: 96: 101: 107) sts.

Work 5 (5: 5: 7: 7: 7) rows.

Dec 1 st as before at side edge of next row and 5 (5: 5: 5: 5: 1) foll 6th (6th: 6th: 6th: 6th: 8th) rows and then, for **XXL size only,** on 4 foll 6th rows. 76 (82: 86: 90: 95: 101) sts

Work 1 (3: 3: 5: 1: 1) rows, end with a WS row.

Shape front slope

Row 1 (RS) (dec): K to last 20 (20: 21: 21: 22: 22) sts, K3tog tbl, yon, K2tog tbl, patt to end.

Short row shaping: MP, patt until 14 (14: 15: 15: 16: 16) sts on right needle, wrap next stitch (by slipping next st to right needle, taking yarn to opposite side of work between needles and then slipping same st back onto left needle – when working back across sts, work the wrapped loop tog with the wrapped st), turn and patt to end.

Row 2: Patt 15 (15: 16: 16: 17: 17) sts, P to end.

Row 3 (RS): K to last 17 (17: 18: 18: 19: 19) sts, yon, K3tog tbl, patt to end.

Short row shaping: Patt until 14 (14: 15: 15: 16: 16) sts on right needle, wrap next stitch, turn and patt to end.

Row 4: Patt 15 (15: 16: 16: 17: 17) sts, P to end.

These last 4 rows form the patt for the horizontal rib collar, with the short row shaping and are worked **throughout.**

Cont on stitches as set, shaping front edge by dec 2 sts every 4th row until 66 (74: 78: 82: 85: 91) sts rem, ending with a **RS** row.

Work 1 row.

Cont to dec at front slope until 8 (12: 12: 14: 14: 16) decs in **all** have been worked and then work decs on every foll 8th row, and **at the same time** shape side and armhole as folls:

Next row (RS) (inc): K2, M1, keeping front neck shaping correct, work to end.

67 (73: 77: 83: 86: 92) sts.

Work 9 rows.

Inc as before at beg of next row and 3 (2: 2: 2: 1: 0) foll 10th rows and then on 0 (1: 1: 1: 2: 3) foll 8th rows.

Work 9 (9: 11: 9: 9: 9) rows, end with a WS row. (Left front should match back to beg of armhole shaping.)

Shape armhole

Keeping front slope shaping correct, cast off 5 sts at beg of next row.

Work 1 row, ending with a WS row.

Dec 1 st at armhole edge on next 3 (3: 3: 3: 3: 5) rows, 2 (3: 3: 4: 5: 5) foll alt rows, and then on 1 (1: 2: 2: 2: 3) foll 4th rows.

Cont to dec at front slope only as set until 32 (33: 36: 37: 39: 40) sts rem.

Cont until left front matches back to start of shoulder shaping, ending with a WS row.

Shape shoulder

Cast off 6 (6: 7: 7: 8: 8) sts, at beg of next row and foll alt row.

Work 1 row.

Cast off 5 (6: 6: 7: 6: 7) sts, inc in next stitch, work to end. 15 (15: 16: 16: 17: 17) sts.

Cont straight for a further 8.5 (8.5: 9: 9: 9.5: 9.5) cm.

Cast off loosely.

RIGHT FRONT

Cast on 168 (180: 188: 196: 206: 218) sts using 2¾ mm (US 2) needles and work as folls:

Row 1 (RS) (dec): (Sl1, P1, psso) to end. 84 (90: 94: 98: 103: 109) sts.

Row 2: Knit.

Row 3: MP, K until 15 (15: 16: 16: 17: 17) sts on right needle, K2tog, yon, K to end.

(Note that a picot is worked at the beg of every RS row along the entire right front opening edge.)

Row 4: Purl.

Row 5: MP, P until 15 (15: 16: 16: 17: 17) sts on right needle, K2tog, yon, P to end.

Row 6: Knit.

The last 4 rows form the horizontal rib and set the stitches for the front edging.

Work 4 (6: 6: 6: 6: 6) more rows in horizontal rib, placing eyelets as before and ending with a WS row.

Next row (RS) (dec): Keeping patt correct, work to last 4 sts, work 2tog tbl, work 2. 83 (89: 93: 97: 102: 108) sts.

Work 3 (1: 1: 1: 1: 1) rows, ending with a WS row.

All sizes

Change to 3¼ mm (US 3) needles.

Next row (RS): Patt 17 (17: 18: 18: 19: 19) sts, K to end.

Next row: P to last 15 (15: 16: 16: 17: 17) sts, patt to end.

These last 2 rows set the stitches.

Cont rep these 2 rows, working 17 (17: 18: 18: 19: 19) sts at front edge as set and rem sts in st st, and **at the same time** cont shaping side as folls:

Work 0 (2: 4: 4: 6: 6) rows, ending with a WS row.

Next row (RS) (dec): Patt 17 (17: 18: 18: 19: 19) sts, K to last 4 sts, K2tog tbl, K2. patt to end. 82 (88: 92: 96: 101: 107) sts.

Work 5 (5: 5: 7: 7: 7) rows.

Dec 1 st as before at side edge of next row and 5 (5: 5: 5: 5: 1) foll 6th (6th: 6th: 6th: 6th: 8th) rows and then, for **XXL size only,** on 4 foll 6th rows.

76 (82: 86: 90: 95: 101) sts

Work 1 (3: 3: 5: 1: 1) rows, ending with a WS row.

Shape front slope

Row 1 (RS) (dec): Patt 17 (17: 18: 18: 19: 19) sts, K3tog, K to end.

Row 2: P to last 15 (15: 16: 16: 17: 17) sts, patt to end.

Short row shaping: MP, patt until 14 (14: 15: 15: 16: 16) sts on right needle, wrap next stitch, turn and patt to end.

Row 3 (RS): Patt 17 (17: 18: 18: 19: 19) sts, yon, K3tog, K to end.

Row 4: P to last 15 (15: 16: 16: 17: 17) sts, patt to end.

Short row shaping: Patt until 14 (14: 15: 15: 16: 16) sts on right needle, wrap next stitch, turn and patt to end.

These last 4 rows form the patt for the horizontal rib collar, with the short row shaping and are worked **throughout.**

Cont on stitches as set, shaping front edge by dec 2 sts every 4th row until 66 (74: 78: 82: 85: 91) sts rem, ending with a **RS** row.

Work 1 row.

Cont to dec at front slope until 8 (12: 12: 14: 14: 16) decs **in all** have been worked and then work decs on every foll 8th row, and **at the same time** shape side and armhole as folls:

Next row (RS) (inc): Work to last 2 sts, M1, K2. 67 (73: 77: 83: 86: 92) sts.

Work 9 rows.

Inc as before at end of next row and 3 (2: 2: 2: 1: 0) foll 10th rows and then on 0 (1: 1: 1: 2: 3) foll 8th rows.

Work 10 (10: 12: 10: 10: 10) rows, ending with a **RS** row.

Shape armhole

Keeping front slope shaping correct, cast off 5 sts at beg of next row.

Dec 1 st at armhole edge on next 3 (3: 3: 3: 3: 5) rows, 2 (3: 3: 3: 4: 5: 5) foll alt rows, and then on 1 (1: 1: 2: 2: 3) foll 4th rows.

Complete as given for left front, reversing shaping.

SLEEVES (both alike)

Note: the sleeves have a short vent at the centre of the lower edge.

First side

Cast on 50 (52: 54: 54: 56: 56) sts using 2¼ mm (US 1) needles.

Row 1 (RS) (dec): (Sl1, K1, psso) to end. 25 (26: 27: 27: 28: 28) sts.

Row 2: Knit.

Row 3: MP, K to end.

Row 4: Knit.

Rep last 2 rows twice more (8 rows in all completed) and ending with a WS row.

Change to 3¼ mm (US 3) needles.

Row 1 (RS): MP, K to end, inc 13 (13: 13: 15: 16: 17) sts evenly across row.

38 (39: 40: 42: 44: 45) sts.

Row 2: P to last 2 sts, K2.

Row 3: MP, K to end.

Rep these 2 rows 2 (2: 3: 3: 4: 4) times more, and then work row 2 again, ending with a WS row.

Next row (RS) (dec): MP, K to last 4 sts, K2 tog tbl, K2. 37 (38: 39: 41: 43: 44) sts.

Work 3 rows, ending with a WS row.

Break yarn and leave sts on a spare needle.

Second side Cast on 50 (52: 54: 54: 56: 56) sts using 2¼ mm (US 1) needles.

Row 1 (RS) (dec): (Sl1, K1, psso) to end. 25 (26: 27: 27: 28: 28) sts.

Row 2: MP, K to end.

Row 3: Knit.

Row 4: Work as row 2.

Rep the last 2 rows twice more (8 rows in all completed) and ending with a WS row.

Change to 3¼ mm (US 3) needles.

Row 1 (RS): K to end, inc 13 (13: 13: 15: 16: 17) sts evenly across row.

38 (39: 40: 42: 44: 45) sts.

Row 2: MP, K1, P to end.

Row 3: Knit.

Rep these 2 (2: 3: 3: 4: 4) rows twice more and then work row 2 again, end with a WS row.

Next row (RS) (dec): K2, K2tog, K to end. 37 (38: 39: 41: 43: 44) sts.

Work 3 rows, ending with a WS row.

Join sides together

Next row (RS): K across 37 (38: 39: 41: 43: 44) sts of second side, then K across 37 (38: 39: 41: 43: 44) sts of first side. 74 (76: 78: 82: 86: 88) sts.

Work 1 row.

Next row (RS) (dec): K2, K2tog, K to last 2 sts, K2tog tbl, K2. 72 (74: 76: 80: 84: 86) sts.

Work 5 rows.

Dec 1 st as before on next row and 3 foll 6th rows, ending with a **RS** row. 64 (66: 68: 72: 76: 78) sts.

Work 19 rows.

Next row (RS) (inc): K2, M1, K to last 2 sts, M1, K2. 66 (68: 70: 74: 78: 80) sts.

Work 15 rows.

Inc as before on next row and 4 foll 16th rows. 76 (78: 80: 84: 88: 90) sts.

Cont straight until sleeve measures 44 (45: 46: 47: 48: 49) cm from top of cuff, ending with a WS row.

Shape sleeve top

Cast off 5 sts at beg of next 2 rows. 66 (68: 70: 74: 78: 80) sts.

Dec 1 st at each end of next 3 rows, then on 1 (1: 1: 2: 2: 2) foll alt rows, and then 7 (8: 8: 9: 9: 9) foll 4th rows. 44 (44: 46: 46: 50: 52) sts.

Work 1 row.

Dec 1 st at each end of next row, then on 2 (2: 2: 1: 1: 3) foll alt rows, and then on 3 foll rows. 32 (32: 34: 36: 40: 38) sts.

Cast off loosely.

MAKING UP

Pin the pieces out, pulling gently to the correct size and shape. Using a steam iron, steam the pieces, but **do not** let the iron touch the knitting at all. Leave for a few seconds to cool, then complete as folls:

Use back stitch or mattress stitch if preferred. Join the shoulder seams.

Join the cast-off edges of the extended fronts together and sew neatly into place around the back neck.

Join sleeve and side seams, leaving a small gap of about 2cm on the right side seam, level with the start of the front neck shaping. Set sleeve top into armhole.

Using a 2.50 mm (US C2) crochet hook, make a button loop on the front edge of cuff. Sew on buttons to correspond with button loops.

Left front tie

With double pointed 2¾ mm (US 2) needles cast on 5 sts.

Row 1 (RS): K5, *without turning work slip these 5 sts to opposite end of needle and bring yarn to opposite end of work pulling it quite tightly across back of these 5 sts, using other needle K these 5 sts again; rep from * until tie is 100 cm long, K5tog and fasten off. With WS of left front facing, pin the end of the tie to the inside edge of the front edging. Stitch firmly into place across the width of the edging.

Right front tie

Work as given for left front tie, until right tie is 120cm long, K5tog and fasten off.

Sew firmly into place on right front as given for left front.

38.5 (41: 43: 45.5: 48: 52) cm (15 (16: 17: 18: 19: 20½) in)

54 (55: 56: 57: 58: 59) cm (21½ (21½: 22: 22½: 23: 23) in)

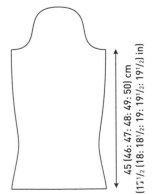

45 (46: 47: 48: 49: 50) cm (17½ (18: 18½: 19: 19½: 19½) in)

IVY

Recommendation

Suitable for the knitter with a little experience.
Please see pages 44 & 45 for photographs.

	XS	S	M	L	XL	XXL	
To fit	**81**	**86**	**91**	**97**	**102**	**109**	**cm**
bust	32	34	36	38	40	43	in

Rowan Kid Classic

	6	7	7	8	8	9	x 50gm

Photoraphed in Bittersweet ᴷ
ᴷ Kim Hargreaves for Rowan

Needles

1 pair 4mm (no 8) (US 6) needles
1 pair 4 ½mm (no 7) (US 7) needles
Cable needle

Tension

23 sts and 28 rows to 10 cm measured
over textured pattern using 4 ½mm (US 7)
needles.

Special abbreviations

C4B = slip next 2 sts onto cable needle and
leave at back of work, K2, then K2 from cable
needle;
C4F = slip next 2 sts onto cable needle and
leave at front of work, K2, then K2 from cable
needle.

BACK

Cast on 97 (103: 109: 115: 119: 129) sts
using 4 ½mm (US 7) needles.
Row 1 (RS): P1 (0: 1: 0: 1: 0), (K1 tbl, P1)
7 (8: 8: 9: 9: 11) times, (K2, P2) 4 times, K2,
P1, (K1 tbl, P1) 15 (17: 19: 21: 22: 24) times,
(K2, P2) 4 times, K2, (P1, K1 tbl) 7 (8: 8: 9:
9: 11) times, P1 (0: 1: 0: 1: 0).
Row 2: K15 (16: 17: 18: 19: 22), P2, (K2, P2)
4 times, K31 (35: 39: 43: 45: 49), P2, (K2,
P2) 4 times, K15 (16: 17: 18: 19: 22).
These 2 rows set the sts – 2 panels of rib with
textured patt between and at sides.
Cont as set for a further 11 rows, ending with
a RS row.
Row 14 (WS): K15 (16: 17: 18: 19: 22), P2,
(K2, M1, P2, M1) 3 times, K2, P2, K31 (35:
39: 43: 45: 49), P2, (K2, M1, P2, M1) 3
times, K2, P2, K15 (16: 17: 18: 19: 22).
109 (115: 121: 127: 131: 141) sts.
Now work in patt as folls:
Row 1 (RS): Patt 15 (16: 17: 18: 19: 22) sts,
K2, P2, K4, C4B, C4F, K4, P2, K2, patt 31
(35: 39: 43: 45: 49) sts, K2, P2, K4, C4B,
C4F, K4, P2, K2, patt 15 (16: 17: 18: 19:
22) sts.
Row 2 and every foll alt row: Patt 15 (16: 17:
18: 19: 22) sts, P2, K2, P16, K2, P2, patt 31
(35: 39: 43: 45: 49) sts, P2, K2, P16, K2, P2,
patt 15 (16: 17: 18: 19: 22) sts.
Row 3: Patt 15 (16: 17: 18: 19: 22) sts, K2,
P2, K2, C4B, K4, C4F, K2, P2, K2, patt 31
(35: 39: 43: 45: 49) sts, K2, P2, K2, C4B,
K4, C4F, K2, P2, K2, patt 15 (16: 17: 18:
19: 22) sts.
Row 5: Patt 15 (16: 17: 18: 19: 22) sts, K2,
P2, C4B, K8, C4F, P2, K2, patt 31 (35: 39:
43: 45: 49) sts, K2, P2, C4B, K8, C4F, P2, K2,
patt 15 (16: 17: 18: 19: 22) sts.
Row 6: As row 2.
These 6 rows form patt.
Cont in patt, shaping side seams by dec 1 st
at each end of 3rd and 4 foll 6th rows.
99 (105: 111: 117: 121: 131) sts.
Cont straight until back measures 24 (24: 25:
25: 25: 25) cm, ending with a WS row.

Inc 1 st at each end of next and 5 foll 8th
rows, taking inc sts into textured patt.
111 (117: 123: 129: 133: 143) sts.
Work 13 (13: 17: 17: 17: 17) rows, ending
with a WS row.

Shape armholes

Keeping patt correct, cast off 5 (5: 5: 5: 5: 6)
sts at beg of next 2 rows.
101 (107: 113: 119: 123: 131) sts.
Dec 1 st at each end of next 5 (5: 5: 7: 7: 7)
rows, then on foll 2 (3: 4: 2: 2: 4) alt rows,
then on foll 4th row.
85 (89: 93: 99: 103: 107) sts.
Cont straight until armhole measures 17 (18:
18: 19: 20: 21) cm, ending with a **RS** row.

Shape back neck

Next row (WS): Patt 27 (27: 29: 30: 31: 33)
sts and turn, leaving rem sts on a holder.
Work each side of neck separately.
Dec 1 st at neck edge of next 3 rows, ending
with a **RS** row.
24 (24: 26: 27: 28: 30) sts.

Shape shoulder

Cast off 7 (7: 8: 8: 9: 9) sts at beg of next
row, dec 1 st at neck edge of foll row, then
cast off 8 (8: 8: 8: 8: 10) sts at beg of foll row.
Work 1 row.
Cast off rem 8 (8: 9: 10: 10: 10) sts.
With **WS** facing rejoin yarn to rem sts, cast
off centre 31 (35: 35: 39: 41: 41) sts, patt to
end. Complete to match first side, reversing
shapings.

LEFT FRONT

Cast on 64 (67: 70: 73: 75: 80) sts using
4 ½mm (US 7) needles.
Row 1 (RS): P1 (0: 1: 0: 1: 0), (K1 tbl, P1) 7
(8: 8: 9: 9: 11) times, (K2, P2) 4 times, K2,
P1, (K1 tbl, P1) 7 (8: 9: 10: 10: 11) times,
P16 (16: 16: 16: 17: 17).
Row 2: K31 (33: 35: 37: 38: 40), P2, (K2, P2)
4 times, K15 (16: 17: 18: 19: 22).
Row 3: P1 (0: 1: 0: 1: 0), (K1 tbl, P1) 7 (8: 8:
9: 9: 11) times, (K2, P2) 4 times, K2, P1, (K1
tbl, P1) 7 (8: 9: 10: 10: 11) times, K16 (16:
16: 16: 17: 17).

Row 4: P16 (16: 16: 16: 17: 17), K15 (17: 19: 21: 21: 23), P2, (K2, P2) 4 times, K15 (16: 17: 18: 19: 22).

These 4 rows set the sts – 1 panel of rib with textured patt either side and front opening edge sts in ridge patt.

Cont as set for a further 9 rows, ending with a RS row.

Row 14 (WS): K31 (33: 35: 37: 38: 40), P2, (K2, M1, P2, M1) 3 times, K2, P2, K15 (16: 17: 18: 19: 22).

70 (73: 76: 79: 81: 86) sts.

Now work in patt as folls:

Row 1 (RS): Patt 15 (16: 17: 18: 19: 22) sts, K2, P2, K4, C4B, C4F, K4, P2, K2, patt 31 (33: 35: 37: 38: 40) sts.

Row 2 and every foll alt row: Patt 31 (33: 35: 37: 38: 40) sts, P2, K2, P16, K2, P2, patt 15 (16: 17: 18: 19: 22) sts.

Row 3: Patt 15 (16: 17: 18: 19: 22) sts, K2, P2, K2, C4B, K4, C4F, K2, P2, K2, patt 31 (33: 35: 37: 38: 40) sts.

Row 5: Patt 15 (16: 17: 18: 19: 22) sts, K2, P2, C4B, K8, C4F, P2, K2, patt 31 (33: 35: 37: 38: 40) sts.

Row 6: As row 2.

These 6 rows form patt.

Cont in patt, shaping side seam by dec 1 st at beg of 3rd and 4 foll 6th rows.

65 (68: 71: 74: 76: 81) sts.

Cont straight until left front measures 24 (24: 25: 25: 25: 25) cm, ending with a WS row.

Shape front slope

Next row (RS): Inc in first st (for side seam inc), patt to last 19 (19: 19: 19: 20: 20) sts, P3tog (for front slope dec), patt to end.

64 (67: 70: 73: 75: 80) sts.

Working all front slope decreases as set by last row, dec 2 sts at front slope edge of 10th and 2 (4: 4: 4: 4: 4) foll 10th rows, then on 1 (0: 0: 0: 0: 0) foll 12th rows and **at same time** inc 1 st at beg of 8th and 4 foll 8th rows.

61 (62: 65: 68: 70: 75) sts.

Work 11 (3: 7: 7: 7: 7) rows, ending with a WS row.

Shape armhole

Keeping patt correct, cast off 5 (5: 5: 5: 5: 6) sts at beg and dec 2 (0: 0: 0: 0: 0) sts at front slope edge of next row.

54 (57: 60: 63: 65: 69) sts.

Work 1 row.

Dec 1 st at armhole edge of next 5 (5: 5: 7: 7: 7) rows, then on foll 2 (3: 4: 2: 2: 4) alt rows, then on foll 4th row and **at same time** dec 2 sts at front slope edge of 11th (5th: next: next: next: next) and foll 0 (10th: 12th: 10th: 10th: 10th) row. 44 (44: 46: 49: 51: 53) sts.

Dec 2 sts at front slope edge **only** on 10th (10th: 8th: 6th: 6th: 2nd) and 1 (1: 1: 2: 2: 2) foll 12th (12th: 12th: 10th: 10th: 10th) rows. 40 (40: 42: 43: 45: 47) sts.

Cont straight until left front matches back to beg of shoulder shaping, ending with a WS row.

Shape shoulder

Cast off 7 (7: 8: 8: 9: 9) sts at beg of next row, cast off 8 (8: 8: 8: 8: 10) sts at beg of foll alt row, then 8 (8: 9: 10: 10: 10) sts at beg of foll alt row. 17 (17: 17: 17: 18: 18) sts.

Cont in patt on these 17 (17: 17: 17: 18: 18) sts only (for back neck border extension) for a further 8 (9: 9: 9.5: 10: 10) cm, ending with a WS row. Cast off.

RIGHT FRONT

Cast on 64 (67: 70: 73: 75: 80) sts using 4 ½mm (US 7) needles.

Row 1 (RS): P16 (16: 16: 16: 17: 17), P1, (K1 tbl, P1) 7 (8: 9: 10: 10: 11) times, (K2, P2) 4 times, K2, (P1, K1 tbl) 7 (8: 8: 9: 9: 11) times, P1 (0: 1: 0: 1: 0).

Row 2: K15 (16: 17: 18: 19: 22), P2, (K2, P2) 4 times, K31 (33: 35: 37: 38: 40).

Row 3: K16 (16: 16: 16: 17: 17), P1, (K1 tbl, P1) 7 (8: 9: 10: 10: 11) times, (K2, P2) 4 times, K2, (P1, K1 tbl) 7 (8: 8: 9: 9: 11) times, P1 (0: 1: 0: 1: 0).

Row 4: K15 (16: 17: 18: 19: 22), P2, (K2, P2) 4 times, K15 (17: 19: 21: 21: 23), P16 (16: 16: 16: 17: 17).

These 4 rows set the sts – 1 panel of rib with textured patt either side and front opening edge sts in ridge patt.

Cont as set for a further 9 rows, ending with a RS row.

Row 14 (WS): K15 (16: 17: 18: 19: 22), P2, (K2, M1, P2, M1) 3 times, K2, P2, K31 (33: 35: 37: 38: 40). 70 (73: 76: 79: 81: 86) sts.

Now work in patt as folls:

Row 1 (RS): Patt 31 (33: 35: 37: 38: 40) sts, K2, P2, K4, C4B, C4F, K4, P2, K2, patt 15 (16: 17: 18: 19: 22) sts.

Row 2 and every foll alt row: Patt 15 (16: 17: 18: 19: 22) sts, P2, K2, P16, K2, P2, patt 31 (33: 35: 37: 38: 40) sts.

Row 3: Patt 31 (33: 35: 37: 38: 40) sts, K2, P2, K2, C4B, K4, C4F, K2, P2, K2, patt 15 (16: 17: 18: 19: 22) sts.

Row 5: Patt 31 (33: 35: 37: 38: 40) sts, K2, P2, C4B, K8, C4F, P2, K2, patt 15 (16: 17: 18: 19: 22) sts.

Row 6: As row 2.

These 6 rows form patt.

Cont in patt, shaping side seam by dec 1 st at end of 3rd and 4 foll 6th rows.

65 (68: 71: 74: 76: 81) sts.

Cont straight until right front measures 24 (24: 25: 25: 25: 25) cm, ending with a WS row.

Shape front slope

Next row (RS): Patt 16 (16: 16: 16: 17: 17) sts, P3tog tbl (for front slope dec), patt to last st, inc in last st (for side seam inc).

64 (67: 70: 73: 75: 80) sts.

Working all front slope decreases as set by last row, complete to match left front, reversing shapings.

SLEEVES (both alike)

Cast on 67 (69: 71: 73: 75: 79) sts using 4 ½mm (US 7) needles.

Row 1 (RS): P1, *K1 tbl, P1; rep from * to end.

Row 2: Knit.

These 2 rows form patt.

Cont in patt for a further 2 (2: 2: 4: 4: 4) rows, ending with a WS row.

Shape top

Keeping patt correct, cast off 5 (5: 5: 5: 5: 6) sts at beg of next 2 rows.

57 (59: 61: 63: 65: 67) sts.

Dec 1 st at each end of next 3 rows, then on foll alt row, then on 4 (5: 5: 5: 5: 6) foll 4th rows, then on foll 4 (4: 4: 4: 5: 5) alt rows, then on foll 5 rows, ending with a WS row.

Cast off rem 23 (23: 25: 27: 27: 27) sts.

MAKING UP

Pin out the pieces and press carefully following instructions on ball band.

Join both shoulder seams using back stitch, or mattress stitch if preferred.

Join cast-off ends of back neck border extensions, then sew one row-end edge in place to back neck edge.

Join side seams.

Join sleeve seams.

Set in sleeves.

Belt
Cast on 10 sts using 4mm (US 6) needles.
Row 1 (RS): K to last 2 sts, inc in next st, K1.
11 sts.
Row 2: P to last 2 sts, P2tog. 10 sts.
Row 3: P to last 2 sts, inc in next st, P1.
11 sts.
Row 4: K to last 2 sts, K2tog. 10 sts.
Rep last 4 rows until belt measures 130
(130: 140: 140: 150: 150) cm, ending
with a WS row.
Cast off.

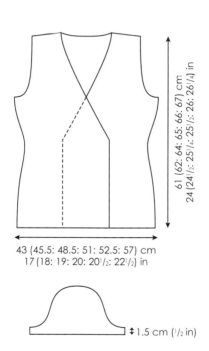

43 (45.5: 48.5: 51: 52.5: 57) cm
17 (18: 19: 20: 20¹/₂: 22¹/₂) in

61 (62: 64: 65: 66: 67) cm
24 (24¹/₂: 25¹/₄: 25¹/₂: 26: 26¹/₄) in

‡ 1.5 cm (¹/₂ in)

Recommendation

Suitable for the novice knitter.

Please see pages 26 & 40 for photographs.

	XS	S	M	L	XL	XXL	
To fit	**81**	**86**	**91**	**97**	**102**	**107**	**cm**
bust	32	34	36	38	40	42	in

Rowan Kid Classic

7	7	8	8	9	10	x 50gm

Photographed in Plush^K / Victoria

^K Kim Hargreaves for Rowan

Needles

1 pair 4 mm (no 8) (US 6) needles
1 pair 4 ½ mm (no 7) (US 7) needles x

Tension

21 sts and 27 rows to 10 cm measured over reversed stocking stitch using 4 ½ mm (US 7) needles.

WHISPER
SWEATER WITH SLASHED NECK & FLOUNCED HEM

BACK

Cast on 250 (258: 278: 290: 306: 318) sts using 4 ½ mm (US 7) needles and work lower flounce as folls:
Row 1 (RS)(dec): *P2 sts, lift 1st st over 2nd st (1 st dec); rep from * to end.
125 (129: 139: 145: 153: 159) sts.
Row 2: Knit.
Beg with a P row, cont in rev st st until work measures 12 (12: 13: 13: 14: 14) cm, ending with a WS row.
Change to 4 mm (US 6) needles.
Next row (RS)(dec): P4 (6: 5: 8: 6: 9) sts, (P3tog, P3) 20 (20: 22: 22: 24: 24) times, P1 (3: 2: 5: 3: 6).
85 (89: 95: 101: 105: 111) sts.
Knit 1 row.
Cont in rev st st shaping sides as folls:
Work 4 rows.
Change to 4 ½ mm (US 7) needles.
Work 10 (10: 10: 10: 12: 12) rows.
Next row (RS)(inc): P2, M1, P to last 2 sts, M1, P2.
87 (91: 97: 103: 107: 113) sts.
Work 11 (11: 11: 11: 13: 13) rows.
Inc 1 st as before at each end of next row and 2 foll 12th (12th: 12th: 12th: 14th: 14th) rows.
93 (97: 103: 109: 113: 119) sts.
Work straight until back measures 25 (25: 26: 26: 27: 27) cm from top of fl ounce, and ending with a WS row.
Shape armholes
Cast off 4 sts at beg of next 2 rows.
85 (89: 95: 101: 105: 111) sts.
Dec 1 st at each end of next 5 (5: 7: 7: 7: 9) rows, then on 3 (3: 3: 4: 5: 4) foll alt rows, and then on foll 4th row.
67 (71: 73: 77: 79: 83) sts.
Work straight until armhole measures 18 (19: 19: 20: 21: 22) cm, ending with a WS row.
Shape shoulders
Cast off 4 (5: 6: 5: 5: 6) sts at beg of next 2 rows and 4 (4: 4: 5: 5: 5) sts beg of foll 4 rows. 43 (45: 45: 47: 49: 51) sts.
Leave sts on a holder.

FRONT

Work as for back.

SLEEVES (work both the same)

Cast on 88 (92: 96: 100: 104: 108) sts using 4 ½ mm (US 7) needles.
Row 1 (RS)(dec): *P2 sts, lift 1st st over 2nd st (1 st dec); rep from * to end.
44 (46: 48: 50: 52: 54) sts.
Row 2: Knit.
Beg with a P row, cont in rev st st shaping sides as folls:
Work 12 rows, ending with a WS row.
Next row (RS)(inc): P2, M1, P to last 2 sts, M1, P2.
46 (48: 50: 52: 54: 56) sts.
Work 11 rows, ending with a WS row.
Inc 1 st as before at each end of next row and 1 (1: 4: 4: 6: 6) foll 12th rows and then every foll 10th row to 64 (66: 68: 70: 72: 74) sts.
Work straight until sleeve measures 44 (45: 46: 47: 48: 49) cm, ending with a WS row.
Shape top
Cast off 4 sts at beg of next 2 rows.
56 (58: 60: 62: 64: 66) sts.
Dec 1 st at each end of next 3 rows, then on 2 foll alt rows, then on every foll 4th row until 38 (40: 42: 44: 46: 46) sts rem.
Work 1 row.
Dec 1 st at each end of next row and 2 (3: 3: 4: 4: 4) foll alt rows, then on every foll row until 22 (22: 24: 24: 26: 26) sts rem.
Cast off.

MAKING UP

Press all pieces using a warm iron over a damp cloth.
Join right shoulder seam using backstitch or mattress stitch if preferred.
Neck edging
With RS of front facing and using 4 mm (US 6) needles, P across 43 (45: 45: 47: 49: 51) sts on holder at front, P across 43 (45: 45: 47: 49: 51) sts on holder at back.
86 (90: 90: 94: 98: 102) sts.

Beg with a knit row, work 8 rows in rev st st.
Cast off knitwise on WS.
Join left shoulder and neckband seam.
Join side and sleeve seams.
Set sleeves into armholes.

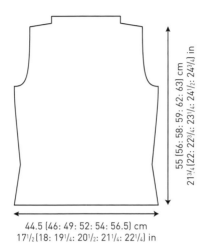

55 (56: 58: 59: 62: 63) cm
21¾(22: 22¾: 23¼: 24½: 24¾) in

44.5 (46: 49: 52: 54: 56.5) cm
17½(18: 19¼: 20½: 21¼: 22¼) in

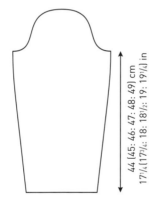

44 (45: 46: 47: 48: 49) cm
17¼(17¾: 18: 18½: 19: 19¼) in

CHARM

CARDIGAN WITH THREE QUARTER OR FULL LENGTH SLEEVE

Recommendation

Suitable for the knitter with a little experience.
Please see page 46 for photograph.

	XS	S	M	L	XL	XXL	
To fit	**81**	**86**	**91**	**97**	**102**	**107**	**cm**
bust	32	34	36	38	40	42	in

Rowan Felted Tweed

| | 7 | 7 | 8 | 8 | 8 | 9 x 50gm |

Photographed in Ancient[K]
[K] Kim Hargreaves for Rowan

Buttons – 6

Needles

1 pair 2¾ mm (no 12) (US 2) needles
1 pair 3¼ mm (no 10) (US 3) needles
1 pair 3¾ mm (no 9) (US 5) needles

Tension

23 sts and 42 rows to 10 cm measured over
garter stitch using 3¾ mm (US 5) needles.

Note: Garter stitch tends to be quite stretchy
when knitted into a large piece so, when
measuring your tension, ensure that the
garter stitch is opened-out a little.

Special abbreviation

MP = Make picot: cast on 1 st, cast off 1 st.
(See information page for details)

BACK

Cast on 99 (105: 111: 117: 121: 127) sts
using 3¼ mm (US 3) needles.
Foundation row (RS): Purl.
Next row: Knit.
Cont in garter stitch, i.e. knit every row,
shaping back as folls:
Work 6 rows, ending with a WS row.
Change to 3¾ mm (US 5) needles.
Work 8 (8: 10: 10: 12: 12) rows, ending with
a WS row.
Place a marker between the 24th (26th: 27th:
29th: 30th: 31st) and 25th (27th: 28th:
30th: 31st: 32nd) sts in from each side.
Next row (RS) (dec): K2, K2tog, K to 2 sts
before marker, K2tog tbl, slip marker onto
right needle, K1, K2tog, K to 3 sts before
second marker, K2tog tbl, K1, slip marker onto
right needle, K2tog, K to last 4 sts, K2tog tbl, K2.
93 (99: 105: 111: 115: 121) sts.
Work 13 (15: 15: 17: 19: 19) rows, taking the
markers up the work on every row.
Dec as before on next row and foll 14th (16th:
16th: 18th: 20th: 20th) row.
81 (87: 93: 99: 103: 109) sts.
Work 27 rows, ending with a WS row.
Next row (RS) (inc): K2, M1, K to marker, M1,
K1, M1, K to second marker, M1, K1, M1, K to
last 2 sts, M1, K2.
87 (93: 99: 105: 109: 115) sts.
Work 17 rows.
Inc as before on next row and foll 18th row.
99 (105: 111: 117: 121: 127) sts.
Cont straight until work measures 32 (32: 32:
34: 34: 35) cm, ending with a WS row.
Shape raglan armholes
Cast off 4 sts at beg of next 2 rows.
91 (97: 103: 109: 113: 119) sts.
Work 4 rows.
Next row (RS) (dec): K2, K3tog, K to last
5 sts, K3tog tbl, K2.
Work 5 rows.
Dec as before on next row, then on 3 (3: 2:
1: 1: 1) foll 6th rows, then on every foll 4th
row until 27 (29: 31: 33: 33: 35) sts rem.
Work 1 row. Cast off.

LEFT FRONT

Cast on 63 (66: 69: 72: 74: 77) sts using
3¼ mm (US 3) needles and work as folls:
Row 1 (RS): Purl.
Row 2: MP, K to end.
Rows 3 & 4 (RS) (Short row shaping): K to
last 15 sts, wrap next stitch (by slipping next
st onto right needle, bringing yarn to front of
work between needles and the slipping same
st back onto left needle), turn and K to end.
Row 5: K to end.
Row 6: P until 15 sts on right needle, K to end.
Row 7 & 8 (Short row shaping): K to last
15 sts, wrap next stitch, turn and K to end.
Change to 3¾mm (US 5) needles.
Row 9: K to last 15 sts, P to end.
Row 10: MP, K to end.
Rows 5, 6, 9 and 10 (omitting the short row
shaping rows) set the sts and row sequence
for the front edging and are repeated up the
entire front, the rem sts are worked in garter
stitch throughout.
Work 6 (6: 8: 8: 10: 10) rows.
Place a marker between the 24th (26th: 27th:
29th: 30th: 31st) and 25th (27th: 28th: 30th:
31st: 32nd) sts in from side edge.
Next row (RS) (dec): K2, K2tog, K to 2 sts
before marker, K2tog tbl, slip marker onto
right needle, K1, K2tog, patt to end.
60 (63: 66: 69: 71: 74) sts.
Work 13 (15: 15: 17: 19: 19) rows, taking the
markers up the work on every row.
Dec as before on next row and foll 14th (16th:
16th: 18th: 20th: 20th) row.
54 (57: 60: 63: 65: 68) sts.
Work 27 rows, ending with a WS row.
Next row (RS) (inc): K2, M1, K to marker, M1,
K1, M1, patt to end. 57 (60: 63: 66: 68: 71) sts.
Work 17 rows.
Inc as before on next row and foll 18th row.
63 (66: 69: 72: 74: 77) sts.
Cont straight until left front matches back to beg
of armhole shaping, ending with a WS row.
Shape raglan armhole
Cast off 4 sts at beg of next row.
59 (62: 65: 68: 70: 73) sts.

Work 5 rows.
Next row (RS) (dec): K2, K3tog, patt to end. 57 (60: 63: 66: 68: 71) sts.
Work 5 rows.
Dec as before on next row, then on 3 (3: 2: 1: 1: 1) foll 6th rows, then on every foll 4th row until 29 (30: 31: 32: 32: 33) sts rem, ending with a **RS** row. ***
Shape front neck
Next row (WS): Patt 23 (24: 25: 26: 26: 27) sts and leave these sts on a holder for collar, work to end. 6 sts.
Work 1 row.
Next row (WS) (dec): Dec 1 st at neck edge, K to end. 5 sts.
Next row (dec): Dec 2 st at armhole edge and 1 st at neck edge. 2 sts.
Next row (dec): K2 tog.
Fasten off.
Mark position of 6 buttons, the first to come 30 (30: 32: 32: 34: 34) rows up from cast-on edge, the last to come 24 (24: 26: 26: 28: 28) rows down from neck edge and rem buttons spaced evenly between.

RIGHT FRONT
Cast on 63 (66: 69: 72: 74: 77) sts using 3¼ mm (US 3) needles and work as folls:
Row 1 (RS): Purl.
Row 2: Knit.
Row 3: MP, K to end.
Rows 4 & 5 (Short row shaping) (WS): K to last 15 sts, wrap next stitch, turn and K to end.
Row 6: K to last 15 sts, P15.
Row 7: P until 15 sts on right needle, K to end.
Row 8 & 9 (Short row shaping) (WS): K to last 15 sts, wrap next stitch, turn and K to end.
Change to 3¾ mm (US 5) needles.
Row 10 (WS): K to end.
Row 11: MP, K to end.
Row 12: K to last 15 sts, P15.
Rows 7, 10, 11 & 12 (omitting the short row shaping rows) set the sts and row sequence for the front edging and are rep up the entire front, the rem sts are worked in garter stitch throughout.
Work 4 (4: 6: 6: 8: 8) rows.
Place a marker between the 24th (26th: 27th: 29th: 30th: 31st) and 25th (27th: 28th: 30th: 31st: 32nd) sts in from side edge.
Cont as for left front to ***, reversing shaping, and at the same time working buttonholes to correspond with markers as folls:
Buttonhole row: Patt 6 sts, work 2tog tbl, (yon) twice, work 2tog, patt to end. (Work into back of loops of yon on the following row.)
Work 1 row, ending with a WS row.
Shape front neck
Next row (RS): Patt 23 (24: 25: 26: 26: 27) sts and leave these sts on a holder for collar, K to end. 6 sts.
Next row (WS) (dec): Dec 1 st at neck edge, K to end. 5 sts.
Next row (dec): Dec 1 st at neck edge and 2 sts at armhole edge. 2 sts.
Next row (dec): K2 tog.
Fasten off.

SLEEVES (both alike)
Three-quarter length sleeve
***Lower edging**
Cast on 12 sts using 3¼ mm (US 3) needles.
Row 1 (RS): Purl.
Row 2: Knit.
Row 3: MP, K to end.
Row 4: Purl.
These 4 rows form the pattern and are rep throughout.**
Cont in pattern until 136 (142: 142: 146: 154: 162) rows have been completed, end with a WS row. Cast off, but do not break yarn.
Upper sleeve
Pick up and knit 68 (70: 72: 74: 78: 82) along the top (straight) edge of lower edging, turn and knit 1 row.
Change to 3¾ mm (US 5) needles and cont in garter st as folls:
Work 68 rows, ending with a WS row.
Next row (RS): K1, M1, K to last st, M1, K1. 70 (72: 74: 76: 80: 84) sts.
Cont in garter st until sleeve measures 34 (35: 36: 37: 38: 39) cm from **lower edge,** ending with a WS row.
Shape raglan
Cast off 4 sts at beg of next 2 rows. 62 (64: 66: 68: 72: 76) sts.
Work 4 rows.
Next row (RS) (dec): K2, K3tog, K to last 5 sts, K3tog tbl, K2.
Work 5 rows.
Dec as before on next row and every foll 6th row until there are 26 (20: 18: 16: 20: 24) sts and then, for **XS, S, M, XL & XXL only,** on every foll 4th row until 10 (12: 14: -: 16: 16) rem, ending with a RS row.
10 (12: 14: 16: 16: 16) sts.
Left sleeve only
Keeping raglan shaping correct, cast off 2 (3: 4: 4: 4: 4) sts at beg of next row, and 3 (3: 4: 5: 5: 5) at beg of foll alt row. 5 (6: 6: 7: 7: 7) sts.
Dec as before on next row.
Cast off rem 3 (4: 4: 5: 5: 5) sts.
Right sleeve only
Work 1 row.
Keeping raglan shaping correct, cast off 2 (3: 4: 4: 4: 4) sts at beg of next row and 3 (3: 4: 5: 5: 5) at beg of foll alt row.
Cast off rem 3 (4: 4: 5: 5: 5) sts.
Full length sleeve
Lower edging
Work given for three-quarter length sleeve from * to **.
Cont in pattern until 98 (102: 106: 110: 118: 126) rows have been completed, ending with a WS row. Cast off, but do not break yarn.
Upper sleeve
Pick up and knit 50 (52: 54: 56: 60: 64) along the top (straight) edge of lower edging, turn and knit 1 row.
Change to 3¾mm (US 5) needles and cont in garter st as folls:
Work 8 rows, ending with a WS row.

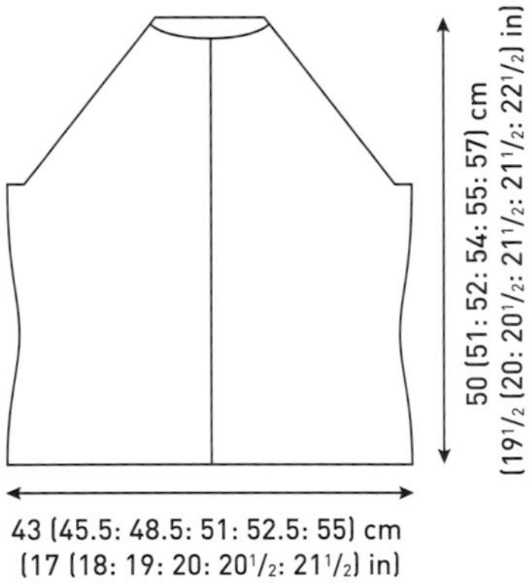
50 (51: 52: 54: 55: 57) cm
(19½ (20: 20½: 21½: 21½: 22½) in)
43 (45.5: 48.5: 51: 52.5: 55) cm
(17 (18: 19: 20: 20½: 21½) in)

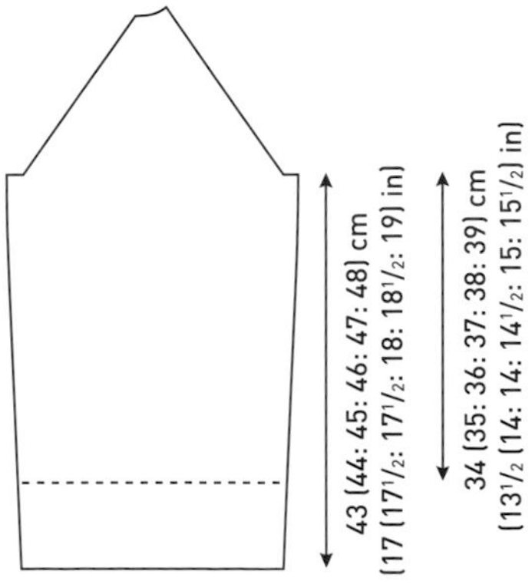
43 (44: 45: 46: 47: 48) cm
(17 (17½: 17½: 18: 18½: 19) in)
34 (35: 36: 37: 38: 39) cm
(13½ (14: 14: 14½: 15: 15½) in)

Continued on following page...

SOUL

SOUCHY HAT IN TWISTED RIB WITH BEADED TRIM

Recommendation

Suitable for the knitter with a little experience.
Please see pages 13, 19 & 25 for photographs.

Two sizes

To fit: small-medium and medium-large

Rowan Kid Classic

    2 x 50gm

Photographed in Bittersweet ᴷ / Teal / Royal
ᴷ Kim hargreaves for Rowan

Beads – 133 (147) x 0.8

Needles

1 pair 4 mm (no 8) (US 6) needles
1 pair 4½ mm (no 7) (US 7) needles

Tension

21 sts and 27 rows to 10 cm measured over
stocking stitch using 4½ mm (US 7) needles.

Special abbreviations

Bead 1 (worked over 3 sts)(RS rows) = place
a bead as folls: P1, now with yarn to front
(RS) of work, slip a bead up next to st just
worked, slip next st purlwise from left needle
to right needle and then P next st, leaving
bead sitting in front of slipped st on RS.

Tw2K = take right-hand needle behind
lefthand needle, skip fi rst st and knit in
back loop of second st, then knit skipped
st through front loop, then sl both sts from
needle together.

Tw2P = take right-hand needle behind
left-hand needle, skip fi rst st and purl in
back loop of second st, then purl skipped
st through front loop, then sl both sts from
needle together.

HAT

Thread 133 (147) beads onto yarn.
Cast on 97 (107) sts using 4 mm (US 6)
needles.
Foundation row (WS): K2, (P2, K3) to end.
Row 1 (RS): (Bead 1, Tw2K) to last 2 sts, P2.
Row 2: K2, (Tw2P, K3) to end.
Rep these last 2 rows 5 times more and then
work row 1 again, ending with a **RS** row.
This completes the bead work.
Next row (WS)(inc): K2, *(yon, P1) twice, K1,
K2tog; rep from * to end. 116 (128) sts.

Change to 4½ mm (US 7) needles.
Row 1 (RS): P2, *K2tog, (yo) twice, sl 1, K1,
psso, P2; rep from * to end.
Row 2: K2, *P1, purl into front of 1st yo, purl
into back of 2nd yo, P1, K2; rep from * to end.
Row 3: P2, *yo, sl 1, K1, psso, K2tog, yo, P2;
rep from * to end.
Row 4: K2, *P4, K2; rep from * to end.
These 4 rows form the pattern and are rep
throughout.
Rep these 4 rows 10 (12) times more and then
work rows 1 – 3 again, ending with a RS row.
Next row (WS)(dec): K2tog, *P4, K2tog; rep
from * to end. 96 (106) sts.
Next row (RS): P1, *K2tog, (yo) twice, sl 1,
K1, psso, P1; rep from * to end.
Next row: K1, *P1, purl into front of 1st yo,
purl into back of 2nd yo, P1, K1; rep from *
to end.
Next row: P1, *yo, sl 1, K1, psso, K2tog, yo,
P1; rep from * to end.
Next row (WS)(dec): K1, *P2tog tbl, P2tog,
K1; rep from * to end. 58 (64) sts.
Next row: P1, (K2, P1) to end.
Next row (WS)(dec): K1, (P2tog, K1) to end.
39 (43) sts.
Next row: P1, (K1, P1) to end.
Next row: (P2tog) to last st, P1. 20 (22)sts.
Break yarn and thread through rem 20 (22) sts.
Pull up tight and fasten off securely. Join seam.

Charm – Continued from previous page...

Next row (RS) (inc): K1, M1, K to last st, M1,
K1. 52 (54: 56: 58: 62: 66) sts.
Work 15 (15: 15: 15: 17: 17) rows.
Inc as before on next row and every foll 14th
(14th: 14th: 14th: 16th: 16th) row until
there are 70 (64: 66: 68: 80: 84) sts and
then, for **S, M & L sizes only,** on every foll
16th row until there are 72 (74: 76) sts.
70 (72. 74: 76: 80: 84) sts.
Cont in garter st until sleeve measures 43
(44: 45: 46: 47: 48) cm from **lower edge,**
ending with a WS row.

Shape raglan

Complete as for three-quarter length sleeve.

MAKING UP

Do not press. Gently steam the pieces using
a warm iron over a damp cloth.
Join the raglan seams using back stitch, or
mattress stitch, if preferred.

Collar

With RS of right front facing and using
2¾mm (US 2) needles, slip 23 (24: 25: 26:
26: 27) sts from holder on to right needle,

pick up and knit 3 sts up front neck, 6 (8: 10:
12: 12: 12) sts across right sleeve, 25 (27:
29: 31: 31: 33) sts across back, 6 (8: 10: 12:
12: 12) sts across left sleeve, 3 sts down left
front neck, then patt across 23 (24: 25: 26:
26: 27) sts from left front holder.
89 (97: 105: 113: 113: 117) sts.
Keeping patt correct over 15 sts at centre
fronts and rem sts in garter st, work 28 (28:
30: 30: 32: 32) rows in patt, ending with a **RS**
row. Cast off knitwise.
Join side and sleeve seams. Sew on buttons.

TRINKET
SCARF WITH RUFFLE TRIM & BEADING DETAIL

Recommendation
Suitable for the knitter with a little experience.
Please see pages 30, 32 & 51 for photographs.

One Size
Rowan Kidsilk Haze
    3 x 25g
Photographed in Fern / Swish

Beads – Approx 656 x 0.8

Needles
1 pair 2¾ mm (no 12) (US 2) needles
1 pair 3¾ mm (no 9) (US 5) needles
1 pair 4 mm (no 8) (US 6) needles

Tension
26 sts and 46 rows to 10 cm measured over
patt using 2¾ mm (US 2) and 4 mm (US 6)
needles.

Finished length
Approximately 173 cm (68 in) long

Special note
Because it is very easy to cast on too
tightly we have done a double cast on
i.e. cast on twice the amount of sts
needed and dec on the first row.

MAIN
Cast on 88 sts using 2¾ mm (US 2) needles.
Row 1 (dec) (RS): (Sl1, K1, psso) to end.
44 sts.
Row 2: Knit to end.
Row 3: K to last 2 sts, inc in next st, K1.
45 sts.
Row 4: K to last 2 sts, K2tog tbl. 44 sts.
Rep the last 2 rows 12 times more (28 rows
in all completed).
Row 29 (RS) (inc): K1, (inc every st) to last
st, K1.
*Change to 4 mm (US 6) needles.
Row 30: K2, P to last 3 sts, K1, K2tog tbl.
Row 31: K to last 2 sts, inc in next st, K1.
Rep the last 2 rows twice more, ending with
a RS row.
Change to 2¾ mm (US 2) needles.
Row 36 (WS) (dec): K1, (P2tog tbl) to last
3 sts, K1, K2tog tbl. 44sts.
Row 37 (RS): K to last 2 sts, inc in next st, K1.
45 sts.
Row 38: K to last 2 sts, K2tog tbl. 44 sts.
Rep the last 2 rows 4 times more.**
Rep from * to ** until scarf measures
approximately 165 cm (65 in), ending with
pattern row 38, then repeat rows 37 and
38 9 times more.
Cast off.

MAKING UP
Do not press
Using a steam iron, steam gently, but **do not**
allow the iron to touch the knitting at all.
Leave for a few seconds to cool, then complete
as folls:
Frills (both ends alike)
Lower frill
With RS facing and using a 2¾ mm (US 2)
needle, pick up and knit 44 sts along short
edge of scarf.
Change to 3¾ mm (US 5) needles.
***Row 1 (WS) (inc): K2, (K in front, P in back
of next stitch) to last 2 sts, K2. 84 sts.
Beg with a K row, work 4 rows in st st, ending
with a WS row.
Row 6 (RS) (inc): K2, (inc every st), to last
2 sts, K2. 164 sts.
Beg with a P row, work 5 rows in st st, ending
with a WS row. 164 sts.
Break yarn.
Thread 164 beads onto the yarn.
Rejoin yarn and cast off as folls: P1 (one loop
on right needle), * wrap the yarn around the
right needle and bring yarn through loop, as if
knitting a st, bring a bead up needle, P1, pass
first stitch on right needle over second st (one
stitch cast off), rep from * to end.
Second frill
With RS facing and lower frill uppermost and
using a 2¾ mm (US 2) needle, pick up and
knit 44 sts along the 8th ridge of the garter st.
Change to 3¾ mm (US 5) needles and
complete as for lower frill from ***.
Work other end to match.

Recommendation

Suitable for the knitter with a little experience.
Please see page 39 for photograph.

	XS	S	M	L	XL	XXL	
To fit	**81**	**86**	**91**	**97**	**102**	**109**	cm
bust	32	34	36	38	40	43	in

Rowan Big Wool

| | 6 | 7 | 8 | 8 | 9 | 10 x 100gm |

Photographed in Eternal[K]
[K] Kim Hargreaves for Rowan

Needles

1 pair 10mm (no 000) (US 15) needles
1 pair 12 mm (US 17) needles

Tension

8 sts and 12 rows to 10 cm measured over
stocking stitch using 12 mm (US 17) needles

Special abbreviation

MP = Make picot: cast on 1 st, cast off 1 st.
(See information page for details)

PAGAN
RAGLAN SWEATER WITH SPLIT COLLAR

BACK
*Lower edging (knitted from side to side)
Cast on 7 (8: 8: 8: 9: 9) sts using 12 mm (US 17)
needles.
Row 1 (RS): MP, K to end.
Row 2: Knit.
Rep these 2 rows until 58 (60: 64: 68: 72: 76)
rows have been completed.
Cast off, but do not break yarn.
Upper back
With RS of lower edging facing and using
12mm (US 17) needles, pick up and knit
34 (36: 38: 40: 42: 46) sts evenly along the
top (straight) edge of edging and purl 1 row,
ending with a WS row.
Beg with a K row, cont in st st as folls:
Work 6 rows.
Next row (RS) (dec): K2, K2tog, K to last 4
sts, K2tog tbl, K2.
32 (34: 36: 38: 40: 44) sts.
Work 5 rows, ending with a WS row.
Dec 1 st as before at each end of next
row.
30 (32: 34: 36: 38: 42) sts.
Work 5 rows, ending with a WS row.
Next row (RS)(inc): K2, M1, K to last 2 sts,
M1, K2.
32 (34: 36: 38: 40: 44) sts. **
Work 7 rows, ending with a WS row.
Inc 1 st as before at each end of next row.
34 (36: 38: 40: 42: 46) sts.
Cont straight until work measures 37.5 (37.5:
38.5: 38.5: 38.5: 37.5) cm from lower edge,
ending with a WS row.
Shape raglan
Cast off 2 sts at beg of next 2 rows.
30 (32: 34: 36: 38: 42) sts.
Work 0 (2: 0: 0: 0: 0) rows.
Next row (RS) (dec): K1, K2tog, K to last
3 sts, K2tog tbl, K1.
28 (30: 32: 34: 36: 40) sts.
M, XL & XXL sizes only
Work 1 row.
Dec 1 st as before at each end of next row
and 0 (0: 1) foll alt row.
30 (34: 36) sts.

All sizes
Work 3 rows, ending with a WS row.
Dec 1 st as before at each end of next row
and every foll 4th row until 20 (22: 22: 24:
24: 26) sts rem.
Work 3 rows, dec 1 (1: 1: 3: 3: 3) sts evenly
across row, and ending with a WS row.
Leave rem 19 (21: 21: 21: 21: 23) sts on a
holder.

FRONT
Work as given for back from * to **.
32 (34: 36: 38: 40: 44) sts.
Work 1 row, ending with a WS row.
Divide for front neck
Next row (RS): K14 (15: 16: 17: 18: 20) sts,
and leave these on a holder for left front,
K to end.
18 (19: 20: 21: 22: 24) sts.
Work on these sts for right front.
Next row: P to last 4 sts, K4.
Next row (RS): MP, K to end.
Next row: P to last 4 sts, K4.
Next row: K to last 2 sts, M1, K2.
19 (20: 21: 22: 23: 25) sts.
This completes the side shaping and set
the sts.
Working 4 sts at centre front in garter st and
rem st in st st, and **at the same time** work a
picot at centre front edge on every alt RS row,
cont as folls:
Cont straight until front matches back
to beg of raglan shaping, ending with a
RS row.
Shape raglan
Cast off 2 sts at beg of next row.
17 (18: 19: 20: 21: 23) sts.
Work 0 (2: 0: 0: 0: 0) rows.
Next row (RS) (dec): Work to last 3 sts, K2tog
tbl, K1. 16 (17: 18: 19: 20: 22) sts.
M, XL & XXL sizes only
Work 1 row.
Dec 1 st as before at end of next row and
0 (0: 1) foll alt row. 17 (19: 20) sts.
All sizes
Work 3 rows, ending with a WS row.

Dec 1 st as before at end of next row and every foll 4th row until 12 (13: 13: 14: 14: 15) sts rem.

Work 3 rows, ending with a WS row.

Do not break yarn.

Leave yarn attached for collar.

Leave sts on a spare needle.

With **WS** facing, cast on 4 sts, rejoin yarn to sts for left front and P to end.

18 (19: 20: 21: 22: 24) sts.

Keeping shaping correct, complete as given for right front, reversing shapings and working a picot at beg of every alt WS row.

Break yarn and leave sts on a spare needle.

SLEEVES (both alike)
*Lower edging (knitted from side to side)

Cast on 7 (8: 8: 8: 9: 9) sts using 12mm (US 17) needles.

Shape side edge

Next row (RS): MP, K until there are 2 (3: 3: 3: 4: 4) sts on right needle, wrap next stitch (by slipping next st to right needle, taking yarn to opposite side of work between needles and then slipping same st back onto left needle – when working back across sts, work the wrapped loop tog with the wrapped st), turn and K to end.

Next row: MP, K until 5 (6: 6: 6: 7: 7) sts on right needle, wrap next stitch, turn and K to end.

Working a picot at beg of every RS row, cont in garter st for a further 36 (38: 40: 40: 42: 44) rows, ending with a WS row.

Shape side edge

Next row: MP, K until 5 (6: 6: 6: 7: 7) sts on right needle, wrap next stitch, turn and K to end.

Next row: MP, K until 2 (3: 3: 3: 4: 4) sts on right needle, wrap next stitch, turn and K to end.

Cast off, but do not break yarn.

Upper sleeve

With RS of lower edging facing and using 12mm (US 17) needles, pick up and knit 22 (23: 24: 25: 26: 27) sts evenly along the top (straight) edge of edging and purl 1 row, ending with a WS row.

Beg with a K row, cont in st st as folls:

Work 2 rows.

Next row (RS) (dec): K2, K2tog, K to last 4 sts, K2tog tbl, K2.

20 (21: 22: 23: 24: 25) sts.

Work 3 rows, ending with a WS row.

Dec 1 st as before at each end of next row.

18 (19: 20: 21: 22: 23) sts.

Work 7 (9: 9: 11: 11: 11) rows, ending with a WS row.

Next row (RS)(inc): K2, M1, K to last 2 sts, M1, K2.

20 (21: 22: 23: 24: 25) sts.

Work 7 rows, ending with a WS row.

Inc as before at each end of next row and foll 8th row.

24 (25: 26: 27: 28: 29) sts.

Cont straight until sleeve measures 46 (47: 48: 49: 50: 51) cm, ending with a WS row.

Shape raglan

Cast off 2 sts at beg of next 2 rows.

20 (21: 22: 23: 24: 25) sts.

Work 0 (0: 2: 2: 2: 2) rows.

Next row (RS) (dec): K1, K2tog, K to last 3 sts, K2tog tbl, K1.

Work 3 rows.

Dec as before on next row and 2 (2: 2: 3: 3: 4) foll 4th row and then every foll alt row until 6 (7: 8: 9: 8: 9) sts rem.

Work 1 row, dec 1 st at centre of row on

M, L & XXL sizes only.

6 (7: 7: 8: 8: 8) sts, and ending with a WS row.

Leave sts on a holder.

MAKING UP

Press all pieces using a warm iron over a damp cloth.

Join raglan seams using back stitch or mattress stitch if preferred.

Collar

With RS facing and using 10mm (US 15) needles, work across 12 (13: 13: 14: 14: 15) sts from right front holder as folls: keeping picot edging correct, K to last 2 sts, K2tog tbl, work across sts from top of right sleeve as folls:

K2tog, K to last 2 sts, K2tog tbl, work across sts from back as folls: K2tog, K to last 2 sts, K2tog tbl, work across sts from top of left sleeve as folls: K2tog, K to last 2 sts, K2tog tbl, work across 12 (13: 13: 14: 14: 15) sts from left front holder as folls: K2tog, K to end.

47 (53: 53: 57: 57: 61) sts.

Next row (WS garment) (RS collar): Keeping picot edge correct, K until 5 sts on right needle, (P1, K1) to last 4 sts, K4.

Cont as set until collar measures 14 (15: 15: 16: 16: 17) cm.

Cast off in pattern.

Join side and sleeve seams.

Neatly slip stitch cast-on sts at base of left front neck in to place behind the right front.

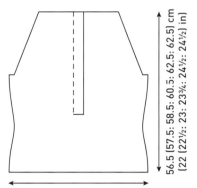

42.5 (45: 47.5: 50: 52.5: 57.5) cm
(16½ (17½: 18½: 19½: 20½: 22½) in)

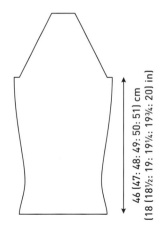

INFORMATION

TENSION

Achieving the correct tension has to be one of the most important elements in producing a beautiful, well fitting knitted garment. The tension controls the size and shape of your finished piece and any variation to either stitches or rows, however slight, will affect your work and change the fit completely. To avoid any disappointment, we would always recommend that you knit a tension square in the yarn and stitch given in the pattern, working perhaps four or five more stitches and rows than those given in the tension note.

When counting the tension, place your knitting on a flat surface and mark out a 10cm square with pins. Count the stitches between the pins. If you have too many stitches to 10cm your knitting it too tight, try again using thicker needles, if you have too few stitches to 10cm your knitting is too loose, so try again using finer needles. Please note, if you are unable to achieve the correct stitches and rows required, the stitches are more crucial as many patterns are knitted to length. Keep an eye on your tension during knitting, especially if you're going back to work which has been put to one side for any length of time.

SIZING

The instructions are given for the smallest size. Where they vary, work the figures in brackets for the larger sizes. One set of figures refers to all sizes. The size diagram with each pattern will help you decide which size to knit. The measurements given on the size diagram are the actual size your garment should be when completed. Measurements will vary from design to design because the necessary ease allowances have been made in each pattern to give your garment the correct fit, i.e. a loose fitting garment will be several cm wider than a neat fitted one, a snug fitting garment may have no ease at all.

WRAP STITCH

A wrap stitch is used to eliminate the hole created when using the short row shaping method. Work to the position on the row indicated in the pattern, wrap the next st (by slipping next st onto right needle, taking yarn to opposite side of work between needles and then slipping same st back onto left needle – on foll rows, K tog the loop and the wrapped st) and turn, cont from pattern.

BEADING

Bead 1 (RS rows) = place a bead by bringing yarn to front (RS) of work and slipping bead up next to st just worked, slip next st purlwise from left needle to right needle and return yarn to back (WS) of work, leaving bead sitting in front of slipped st on RS. Do not place beads on edge sts of rows as this will interfere with seaming and picking up sts.

Beading note

Before starting to knit, thread beads onto yarn. To do this, thread a fine sewing needle (one which will easily pass through the beads) with sewing thread. Knot ends of thread and then pass end of yarn through this loop. Thread a bead onto sewing thread and then gently slide it along and onto knitting yarn. Continue in this way until required numbers of beads are on yarn.

WORKING A LACE PATTERN

When working a lace pattern it is important to remember that if you are unable to work a full repeat i.e. both the increase and corresponding decrease and vice versa, the stitches should be worked in stocking stitch or an alternative stitch suggested in the pattern.

CHART NOTE

Some of our patterns include a chart. Each square on a chart represent a stitch and each line of squares a row of knitting.

When working from a chart, unless otherwise stated, read odd rows (RS) from right to left and even rows (WS) from left to right. The key alongside each chart indicates how each stitch is worked.

FINISHING INSTRUCTIONS

It is the pressing and finishing which will transform your knitted pieces into a garment to be proud of.

Pressing

Darn in ends neatly along the selvage edge. Follow closely any special instructions given on the pattern or ball band and always take great care not to over press your work.

Block out your knitting on a pressing or ironing board, easing into shape, and unless otherwise states, press each piece using a warm iron over a damp cloth.

Tip: Attention should be given to ribs/edgings; if the garment is close fitting – steam the ribs gently so that the stitches fill out but stay elastic. Alternatively if the garment is to hang straight then steam out to the correct shape.

Tip: Take special care to press the selvages, as this will make sewing up both easier and neater.

CONSTRUCTION

Stitching together

When stitching the pieces together, remember to match areas of pattern very carefully where they meet. Use a stitch such as back stitch or mattress stitch for all main knitting seams and join all ribs and neckband with mattress stitch, unless otherwise stated.

Take extra care when stitching the edgings and collars around the back neck of a garment. They control the width of the back neck, and if too wide the garment will be ill fitting and drop off the shoulder. Knit back neck edgings only to the length stated in the pattern, even stretching it slightly if for example, you are working in garter or horizontal rib stitch.

Stitch edgings/collars firmly into place using a back stitch seam, easing-in the back neck to fit the collar/edging rather than stretching the collar/edging to fit the back neck.

Straight cast-off sleeves: Place centre of cast-off edge of sleeve to shoulder seams. Sew top of sleeve to body, using markers as guidelines where applicable. Join side and sleeve seams.

Set-in sleeves: Join side and sleeve seams. Place centre of cast off edge of sleeve to shoulder seams. Set in sleeve, easing sleeve head into armhole.

CARE INSTRUCTIONS
Yarns
Follow the care instructions printed on each individual ball band. Where different yarns are used in the same garment, follow the care instructions for the more delicate one.

Buttons
We recommend that buttons are removed if your garment is to be machine washed.

ABBREVIATIONS

K	knit
P	purl
K1b	knit 1 through back loop
st(s)	stitch(es)
inc	increas(e)(ing)
dec	decreas(e)(ing)
st st	stocking stitch (1 row K, 1 row P)
garter st	garter stitch (K every row)
beg	begin(ning)
foll	following
rem	remain(ing)
rev st st	reverse stocking stitch (1 row P, 1 row K)
rep	repeat
alt	alternate
cont	continue
patt	pattern
tog	together
mm	millimetres
cm	centimetres
in(s)	inch(es)
RS	right side
WS	wrong side
sl 1	slip one stitch
psso	pass slipped stitch over
tbl	through back of loop
M1	make one stitch by picking up horizontal loop before next stitch and knitting into back of it
M1p	make one stitch by picking up horizontal loop before next stitch and purling into back of it
yfwd	yarn forward
yon	yarn over needle
yrn	yarn round needle
Mp	Make picot: Cast on 1 st, by inserting the right needle between the first and second stitch on left needle, take yarn round needle, bring loop through and place on left (one stitch cast on), cast off 1 st, by knitting first the loop and then the next stitch, pass the first stitch over the second (one stitch cast off).
Cn	cabl needle
C4B	Cable 4 back: Slip next 2 sts onto a cn and hold at back of work, K2, K2 from cn.
C4F	Cable 4 front: Slip next 2 sts onto a cn and hold at front of work, K2, K2 from cn.

ACKNOWLEDGEMENTS

Kathleen and I would like to say a big thank you to everyone of our fantastic team; we couldn't have produced this wonderful book without you. As always to Graham, his brilliance in both photography and editorial design - Angela, for her skillfulness on the page layouts - our five most beautiful models, Amanda, Nichola, Louise, Sally and Hannah - to Diana who again created the wonderful hair and make-up throughout, and also to her and Peter for the loan of the great props - Sue and Stella for their pattern writing expertise - Susan for her patience in finishing the garments, and our brilliant knitters, Arna, Sandra, Ella, Betty, Mary and Glennis.

Finally, our very special thanks go to Kevin, Rachel, Peter, Paul and all at Cliffe House for allowing us to shoot at such an extraordinary location and making us feel so welcome.

INDEX